Personal Journey

Personal Journey

John Zaradin
in Conversation with
Hephzibah Yohannan

at

Chemin de Guitardou

Cambon d'Albi

France

Melchisedec Press

Melchisedec Press

5 Taylor Road, Altrincham, Cheshire WA14 4LR UK
melchisedecpress.net
info@melchisedecpress.net

Published in the UK in 2015 by Melchisedec Press

Edited by John Zaradin, Hephzibah Yohannan and Robin Miksad 2015

The rights of John Zaradin and Hephzibah Yohannan to be identified as co-authors of this work has been asserted by them in accordance with Copyrights Designs and Patents Act

© 2015 John Zaradin and Hephzibah Yohannan

All rights reserved. No part of this book may be used, edited, transmitted in any form or by any means (electronic, mechanical, photocopying, recording or otherwise), or reproduced in any manner without permission except in the case of brief quotations embodied in reviews or articles. It may not be lent, resold, hired out or otherwise circulated without the publisher's permission.

Permission can be obtained through Melchisedec Press.
The moral rights of the authors are asserted.

Please purchase only authorized editions, and do not participate in or encourage electronic piracy of copyrighted materials. Your support of the author's rights is appreciated.

This book is sold subject to the condition that it shall not, by way of trade or otherwise, be lent re-sold, hired out or otherwise circulated without the publisher's prior consent in any form of binding or cover other than that in which it is published and without a similar condition including this condition being imposed on the subsequent purchaser.
Making or distributing electronic copies of this book constitutes copyright infringement.

ISBN 978-1-872240-29-9 (hardback)

ISBN 978-1-872240-30-5 (paperback)

ISBN 978-1-872240-31-2 (ebook)

Printed and bound by IngramSpark

Set in Baskerville

'Personal Journey'

– is for readers who would reflect on, understand and come to terms with the contents of their own minds.

– is for those who choose to know, savour and value internal personal freedom.

"Personal Journey"

is dedicated, in memoriam, to Noëlle Zaradin for her continued, constant and encouraging support during our thirty three years together.

JZ

CONTENTS

PRELUDE

	Foreword	
	Preface	1
	Personal Journey: *Location of conversation*	2
	Introduction by Hephzibah Yohannan	5
	Prelude to Easter Song: *Guitar solo*	10

CHAPTER

1:	Prelude: *Waiting for a guitar*	12
	First meeting	13
2:	Memory Patterns: *Notes on memory*	16
3:	Remembering Memories: *Meeting Eugene Halliday*	20
4:	Defining Terms	24
5:	The Guitar	30
6:	Tuition in Music	40
7:	Joseph Schillinger: *Theories of Music*	46
8:	Musical Space Time Power	58
9:	To Be or Not To Be: *Determining a life*	64
10:	Don Lord	74
11:	Ishvalian Overtures	80
12:	Preparation for the Road	86
13:	Making a Way Near and Far	90
14:	Universal to Particular	98
15:	Coda	106
	Easter Song: *Lead line & Guitar Accompaniment*	114
	Eugene Halliday: *Biographical notes*	117
16:	Personal Reflections on a Personal Journey	118

POSTCRIPT

Glossary 127

Acknowledgements 142

PHOTOGRAPHS AND GRAPHICS

Bach, J.S: 41.

Chemin de Guitardou: 2, 3, 57, 90, 118.

Halliday, Eugene & works: 9, 10, 11, 15, 29, 59, 79, 83, 95, 100, 112, 113, 114, 115, 116, 124.

Lord, Don: 74, 78, 79.

Mozart, W.A: 52.

Miscellaneous Photographs & Images: Lobes of the brain 16. Camel 24. Definers of terms 25. Sound production 28, 29. 'Birdcage' 30, Frankfurt Musik Messe 36, 37, 57. Music graphs 53, 56. Guitar bracings 63. Voice leading charts 71, 72, 73. Wellington Road 80. Pegasus case 107.

Music: 10, 11, 40, 56, 71, 72, 73, 114, 115, 116.

Musical Instruments: Guitar Hohner 23. Guitar Stephan Schlemper Kompakt Classic 31. Guitar SoloEtte 36. Guitar Godin Multiac 38. Guitar 4 string 84. Violin 84. Napolitan Mandolin 85. Guitar Ovation Legend 98.

Schillinger, Joseph: 47.

Segovia by *Theresa McAllister* 39.

Yohannan, Hephzibah: 3, 8, 78.

Zaradin, John: 4, 12, 13, 20, 37, 45, 57, 62, 64, 65, 81, 86, 87, 91, 101, 106, 119.

Zaradin, Noëlle & works: 91, 96, 97, 101, 103, 104, 105, 125, 126.

The images in this book are taken from a variety of sources: old photographs, new photographs, stills from videos and a variety of graphics and music notation. This means that, although we would have preferred otherwise, the overall quality is variable.

FOREWORD

NOTES ON SOUND, SENSE AND GRAPHICS

If, when we speak or listen to someone else speaking, we choose to focus on the sounds of the letters heard, rather than on the concepts or ideas that those combinations of letters conjure up in our minds, we can listen to those sounds, their vibrations, internal rhythms and partials as we listen to music. We can hear and feel phrasing, dynamics and pitch variations without the intellect interpreting those sounds and creating a fixed idea.

When we put sounds together as words, phrases and sentences, our purpose, generally, is to define ideas and communicate with another person; we wish to express that purpose objectively and clearly.

When we give ourselves to listen to or play music, the dynamic is to a personal involvement, which centres us in ourselves; we live in the moment, listening without regard to any *a priori* purpose. When we feel the actuality of music, well structured and played, we live and breathe the expression of it as it happens, we become at one with it and ourselves. Although appreciation of music by a musically trained mind is enhanced by an intellectual clarity of understanding of the forms and their relationships, there is no necessity to be so trained to be at one with and enjoy that music.

If we open ourselves up to the values in works of art we can find ourselves in the experience of balancing the polarized dynamics of detachment and involvement, of knowing and feeling at the same time. We are lead to reflect onto our own centres and, as individuals, gain insights into our natural authority and sense of freedom. At the same time, we feel a sense of universality, of well being with the world and *know* that our experience is one that is shared and can be understood by others. Because we *know* that our experience is shared, we can more easily accept the variety, diversity and apparent contradictions of the world and be at one with them.

I see the work of Eugene Halliday to be such real artistic work that opens up the mind to an understanding of non-dual individual and universal expression. It explains specifically how to arrive at this authoritative centring and understanding, with nothing more needed than a will to see life as it is and accept it so.

The more I reflect on my personal experiences with Eugene Halliday the more I listen to the sound of sense, try to understand the sense in sound and live with that balancing of the particular and the universal.

Personal Journey includes photographs and graphics with captions, which relate directly to persons mentioned in the text and add visual emphasis to ideas raised. They offer the reader some orientation to the persons, places and ideas under discussion.

I am moved by the forms of musical instruments and include photographs of personal guitars with a brief description of the function of each in different music settings. Also included is a selection of instruments belonging to and played by Eugene Halliday.

The symbols - ♃ ♄ ☿ - are graphics for the planets Jupiter, Saturn, Mercury and serve as reminders that energy of the life force directed to the expression and realization of music continually expands, contracts and spins, creating interest anew.

If the reading of this book can sow a seed of the idea or lead to an intuition, for even one person, that such insight and interest in his work could be valuable, then the production of it will have been worthwhile.

John Zaradin

PREFACE

In everyday life, our attention is drawn out of itself to focus on events which we have not consciously originated and over which there is very little control. If we do not continually ask ourselves what we are doing and why, we risk forgetting that we have within ourselves a capacity for free choice and autonomous action.

Personal Journey reminds the reader of this capacity through the story of John Zaradin's experience of meeting Eugene Halliday and other individuals who believed that a sense of well being, good health and positive approach to life's difficulties are found in good willed inter-relations, a cultivation of fine feeling and clear thinking.

The basic viewpoint is that we are, as individuals, fundamentally responsible for ourselves and what we do. If we do not like what we are doing we can examine our likes, dislikes, motives and ideas and by will cause our situations and conditions to change.

It is hoped that this book will stimulate the reader to look into his or her own personal treasure chest.

How can we deal with the rapidly increasing pace and complexity of life, fear of terrorism and the threatening state of world affairs, impending ecological destruction and the confusions of personal relationships—without succumbing to the wear and tear of stress, to depression and illness?

In his writings, particularly in his book *Reflexive Self-Consciousness*, Eugene Halliday sets out a solution, a way by which we can develop the ability to respond adequately to the demands life makes of us, the ability to assimilate the shocks and blows of experience, so we can live a whole and balanced life. The way to this balance is through an understanding of the centre of our own being, our consciousness, and through this, finding our place in the world.

Personal Journey

Personal Journey
Location of conversation

View from the terrace of Chemin de Guitardou as seen by Hephzibah Yohannan during her Personal Journey conversations with John Zaradin

In the garden where the conversations began

Personal Journey

Walking on the wild side

Personal Journey

John Zaradin in concert

taken by a listener on a Japanese charter cruise.

> "The man that hath no music in himself,
> Nor is not moved with concord of sweet sounds,
> Is fit for treasons, stratagems, and spoils;
> The motions of his spirit are dull as night,
> And his affections dark as Erebus.
> Let no such man be trusted. Mark the music."
>
> William Shakespeare, *The Merchant of Venice*

Personal Journey

Introduction
by
Hephzibah Yohannan

Welcome to this *Personal Journey*, one of a series of conversations with people who knew the artist and writer Eugene Halliday. Here, I introduce my friend John Zaradin, guitarist, composer and explorer of languages, who has agreed to share his story with us and make this recapitulation of his life-journey.

John and I both grew up in Manchester, and we share an interest in music. He had a head start—when we first became aware of each other, I was still at school, while he was on the threshold of his musical career.

Eugene Halliday had been teaching and lecturing for a number of years in Manchester and Liverpool, and, with Ken Ratcliffe, in the 1950s, had founded the International Hermeneutic Society, or IHS. A few years later, in the 1960s, Eugene, in company with the Liverpool philanthropist Fred Freeman and the actor David Mahlowe, founded the charity, the Institute for the Study of Hierological Values. There, Eugene continued to teach and give monthly lectures on many topics including art, religion, philosophy, science and music.

Through a chance meeting—of which more later—John and a friend came into the circle which had gathered around Eugene; I was already there, having grown up in that community. It is through that connection that we have come to share another, vital, interest—the ideas and work of Eugene Halliday.

I am working on a biography of Eugene, and in the course of a chance conversation, John kindly invited me to stay in his house in France, with the purpose of recording a conversation about how he had met Eugene, and about the influence which Eugene had on his life and development. Taking myself and a number of friends by surprise, I took John at his word and, with uncharacteristic alacrity, hopped onto a 'plane to Toulouse at short notice. I really didn't want to miss the opportunity of a conversation with John. I had known him a for a long time, and knew he had made a most interesting life for himself; but, as I came to realise, I didn't know him at all well.

On my return home from France I was taken by surprise again—by John. I was sending him transcripts, by installment, of our conversation. He began to re-work the content, turning it into a far more interesting and valuable creation than I could possibly have anticipated. He also had many ideas of how to present the material—first an e-book, maybe a performance, possibly a video.

Thus it is, that after many further hours conversation, on Skype, we find ourselves still talking, and bringing John's own particular Personal Journey to a new audience.

Why are we talking about Eugene Halliday?

Well, I think John would agree that we feel that our own lives could not have been as they are, without him. We believe that the principles Eugene taught continue to be vital, relevant, worth remembering, and worth sharing.

When one met Eugene for the first time, there would be an immediate rapport; he was 'present' in a way that few people are. Whatever one discussed or did with him would lay bare one's inefficiencies, clarify one's will and intent, and send one away inspired to change one's patterns of behaviour.

On meeting Eugene, a person might simply have a question about business, or some other matter, and, having listened to what he had to offer, would leave to put into practice what they had learned.

On the other hand, a meeting with him could bring into consciousness a hidden intent, a discomfiting realization which might lead that person to depart, never again to reappear.

Most who met Eugene, however, would feel it beneficial to engage with him, and through this interaction would learn how to develop their potential and to succeed, each in his or her own way. One would feel 'lifted' to have been with him and be filled with determination to continue life with positivity and with purpose.

Of all those who knew Eugene personally, I do not think there is one who would deny that he was a remarkable human being, a man who affected for the better and inspired the positive development of many lives.

I have had the good fortune to meet several such people. From them I have learned of how they met Eugene, and of the transformative effect he had on their lives. Those who knew Eugene may well find that these personal accounts resonate with their own experiences. Those who never met him, or had never even heard of him before, will, I hope, find much to interest them and even inspire them to explore his written and spoken legacy.

A good description of meeting Eugene can be found in the autobiography of Maurice Clegg. He described the way Eugene related to those he met: Eugene "never sought to change anyone's opinions or ideas—all he did was to ask questions. But they tended to be ones that couldn't be answered from within the existing belief structure of the party concerned. This required that one had either to pretend the question hadn't been put, or to modify one's position to accommodate it." Maurice went on to say, "And so began the opening of my mind to a sense of the wholeness of life, of an undivided source of all, of its interlocking character, and ultimately its unity. Sectarian and denominational exclusivity evaporated. It was breathtaking stuff, the influence and ongoing evolution of which remains."

I am most grateful to Bob Hardy, founder and administrator of the online Eugene Halliday Archive, for initiating this series of interviews with people who knew Eugene. In 2005, he proposed and undertook an 'Ethnographic Study', conducted through interviews with a number of people whom he saw as having some sort of connection, or 'relationship', with Eugene. For a number of reasons, Bob subsequently called a halt to his project; however, he felt that the content of the interviews was both interesting and valuable, and he allowed me to publish them in the Halliday Review, with the consent of the participants.

I began, gradually, to realise the importance of the work which Bob had done, and it became clear to me that the interviews which he had conducted could be, in addition to their ethnographic value, ideal source material for a biography. I felt it would be good to do more interviews, and so I approached a number of friends who had known Eugene for many years. They very kindly agreed to speak with me, on record. I began to think of the interviews, as 'conversations', and, as each person had a most interesting story to tell in their own right, began to call them 'personal journeys'. Later, I realised that the interviews, or conversations, were, in fact, an oral history of Eugene Halliday, his work, the community of people who had gathered around him, and the times in which they lived.

I am most grateful to those who have spoken with me so far; and grateful to Bob and to those who agreed to be interviewed by him. These conversations throw valuable light on Eugene's character and his modus operandi, which I hope will be of interest to those who come to study his work in future.

By telling his story, in part through the recollections of those who knew him, I hope to introduce new people to Eugene, showing the kind of person he was and how valuable his work still is. In addition, I have found during the conversations, that every person I have spoken to has a story to tell which is valuable in its own right, and each person is worthy of our respect. It is a privilege to have spoken with them all, and to have spoken with John Zaradin, to hear his unique story.

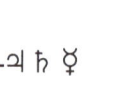

Personal Journey

Eugene Halliday by Zero Mahlowe

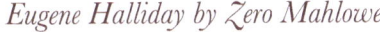

Personal Journey

The theme 'Easter Song' composed by Eugene Halliday is here arranged as a Prelude for Solo Guitar

Personal Journey

Personal Journey

Chapter 1

Prelude

Waiting for a guitar

John Zaradin younger than now.

Personal Journey

First Meeting and Impressions

of

Eugene Halliday

"There are chance meetings with strangers that interest us from the first moment, before a word is spoken."

Fyodor Dostoyevsky, Crime and Punishment

On a personal journey with a guitar

Still younger than now.

HY: The *Personal Journey* of John Zaradin, Zan as he was familiarly known at the time that we first met, has brought him to Chemin de Guitardou, Cambon d'Albi in France.

You are one of those who, as a teenager, knew Eugene Halliday and have said that on first meeting him thought him to be about a hundred years old.

JZ: In retrospect maybe a thousand years; ageless would be closer to what I felt.

Whenever I was with him I felt timelessly well, without anything needing to be said. His age did not seem to matter.

HY: I understand that you and John Resek, the violinist, were among those who attended Eugene's lectures in Liverpool?

JZ: Yes. We had met Don Lord, a friend of Eugene from the Manchester School of Art, and who arranged our introductions to him. Each month we drove to Liverpool with Don to listen to Eugene speak.

HY: Could you tell your own story of being introduced to him?

JZ: It was Don Lord who understood that I was struggling to find a way of becoming a professional musician and suggested that I talk to Eugene.

He arranged a meeting for us and, on sight, I adopted Eugene as a father figure. I accepted him as someone trustworthy and with authority and felt that, by listening to what he said, I might some time soon have a life in music.

From him I started to learn about quiet persistence and began to realise that while life does not always give one what one wants, it does produce what one needs.

HY: Could you enlarge on that?

JZ: We would need to look at a time before meeting Eugene.

Personal Journey

At the age of thirteen, I was stunned by the impact of discovering music with the guitar and felt something that I had not experienced before; it was so different from anything else, took me by surprise and absorbed me completely. Thereafter, life started to become complicated.

♃ ♄ ☿

Intuited drawing by Eugene Halliday of John Zaradin's closest relative by temperament.

Personal Journey

Chapter 2

Memory Patterns

Notes on Memory

"Human protoplasm is a super-sensitive recording material which records the experiences of its surrounding conditions even in utero."

"Without memory we could not even re-cognize ourselves."

Eugene Halliday

Pattern recognition occurs when one comprehends connections between various stimuli and then identifies those connected stimuli as a unity. It is an innate ability of animals. Of the four lobes in the brain: Frontal, Parietal, Occipital and Temporal, it is the temporal (green) lobe that is involved in the retention of visual memories, processing sensory input, comprehending language, storing new memories, emotion, and deriving meaning.

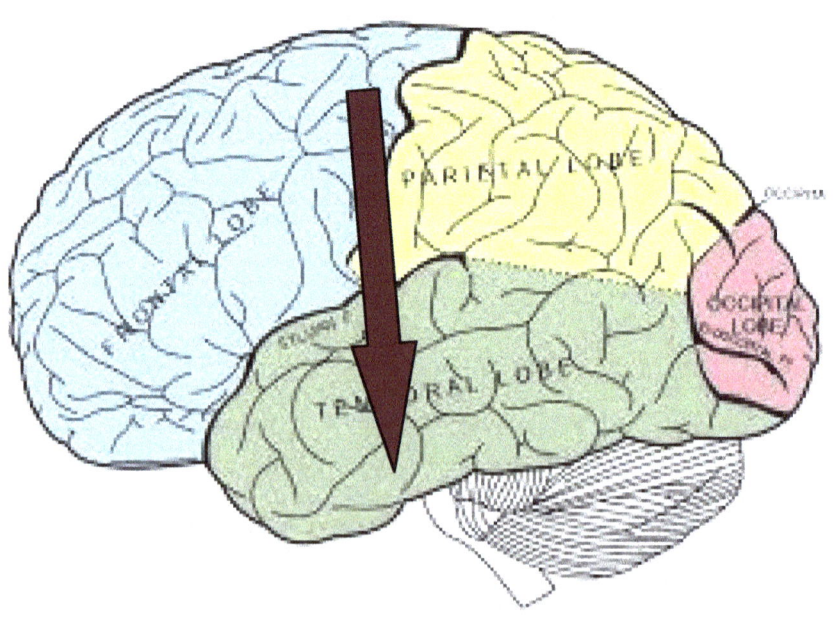

HY: So, let us go to the beginning of a life that became complicated.

JZ: At the beginning, we would remind ourselves that the value of describing to others, details of an individual life, is to show that there are principles functioning in those details, which are shared in all lives.

The individual life force, which created those details, can become lost in its personal choices and forget that each and every other individual, in a unique way breathes and suffers the same joys and sadnesses, hopes and disappointments, dynamics of sickness and health, etc.

Each of us has a story to tell, the details of which, positively presented, can inspire another to look to the understanding of and actualizing of freedom in his or her own own life.

Although the personal choices made by each individual produce very different outcomes in life, there are therein principles operating, which are recognized and shared by everyone.

Discussing and detailing our individual histories can free us of attachment to them and let us see operating, beyond our personal distractions, those universal common principles of which, in varying degrees of sensitivity, we are all conscious.

The keys to understanding each individual history are held in the memories of that individual.

HY: Let us look at memory patterns.

JZ: A memory pattern, or engram, is a recording of stimuli experienced by a person. It is similar to a recording that is saved to a hard disk by a computer but includes emotions and moods felt at the time of the stimuli. The techniques of reading these patterns allow a person to review and then free him or herself from the conditioning caused by enslaving effects of nervous energy locked into those patterns. With a normal computer hard disk erasure the disk retains a light imprint of the pattern erased, which can be read later if necessary. Organic memory patterns are again similar in that they can be erased, but likewise, retain a light imprint. The difference between a hard disk recording and a neural-organic memory is that when an organic memory pattern is erased it releases constrained emotional energy. The person feels, with the release of this energy, liberated and to have increased internal space, as indeed more space is also created on a hard disk. He or she feels free from that memory conditioning and in a detached state is able to review and rebalance him or herself with regard to the decisions taken which led to the energy being encapsulated in the first place.

During many of the sessions that I had alone with Eugene we searched for, found and examined memories which were negative determinants in my life. A sensitive question from him would open up a door into the past and we would explore the significances of these memories until they ceased to control how I felt.

The technique of Eugene was to induce relaxation by his deliberately becoming quiet and then to ask what I was seeing and then how I felt about what I was seeing.

His art was to sense the importance of any reply or movement that I made, to feel tension and tone in the voice and appreciate the timing of the response. As I relaxed, listening to the tone of Eugene's voice and his questions, I became completely absorbed by internal activity and ceased to be aware of physical time and place; I found myself more and more centred in calm feeling. At each stage he would ask what my feelings were, and after my reply, would pose another question. At a certain point the essence of a memory which had become problematic for me would show itself. By entering the memory its significance with respect to will and intention would be understood. The replaying of the memory, in this way, loosened its hold on the mind and freed the feeling locked in by it; that to which I had been unconsciously attached was seen in a new light. Eugene, sensing that the tensions of the problem had ceased to be a determining factor, would gently guide me back to the present real time and place. The overall effect was to be awakened from a sleep during which I had not been asleep; I felt free, whole and well.

The techniques of engram or memory reading allow a person to review and unlock the nervous energy of organically recorded patterns, which are anti-life and debilitating, and free him or her from them. At the same time the memory of the decisions, which led to the energy being locked in the first place, is understood and retained.

Essential to the unlocking is the reviewing and redefining of the events with words correctly applied.

Although at first this release leaves one feeling quite dis-orientated, after a few sessions, one learns to adjust to it and to prefer that detached free-dome state rather than the restrictive feelings produced by identification.

If ever a proof were needed to show that the essence of life is not a material object then for me this would be it; to release nervous energy that has been locked in and then freed by my will is the same as awakening from a deep sleep and feeling reborn.

HY: Then let us next look at some of your earliest memories.

♃ ♄ ☿

Personal Journey

Chapter 3

Remembering Memories

John Zaradin and John Resek as the Zanek Duo

On the beat but ahead of their time. The photo above pre-dates a summer season of "Sunday Concerts at the Ocean Room Blackpool Tower, Blackpool. Below post-dates the same season

Personal Journey

The Beginning of the Journey

"If music be the food of love, play on,
Give me excess of it; that surfeiting,
The appetite may sicken, and so die."

William Shakespeare, Twelfth Night Act 1, scene 1, 1–3

HY: Let us go to your earliest memories. When were you born?

JZ: 22nd May 1943.

It was wartime and we lived close to the Pennine Hills, on the east side of Manchester, in an area which was spared the direct bombing suffered by both Manchester and Liverpool but did receive stray bombs and some damage. I have clear memories of warning sirens, being carried about in a baby gas mask box, often into an air raid shelter at a large nearby house. I can still recall the bombing noises and shrapnel pinging on pavements and walls, the engine noise of planes and the whistling of flying bombs; the dark red sky and smell of burning. The "all clear" sirens, indicating that the bombing had stopped for that night, relieved everyone of his and her fears of not surviving the night. Although, as a child, there was no understanding of what was happening, those early impressions and associated moods retain an awareness of continual fear and then relief which everyone was feeling at the time. They remain as clear memories to this day.

HY: Fear and then relief, compression and decompression.

JZ: Looking back, I am sure that I could be forgiven for thinking that being born at that moment in time had not been such a good idea.

Probably one of the reasons that the South of France seemed so attractive when I first came here, was that it was a very beautiful place with mountains, open countryside and rivers, so contrasting with my early memories of bomb-sites, shelters and rats.

21

It must be said that there was great excitement as a child going into bombed buildings, ignoring "Danger Keep Out" signs, which were placed as a warning that the building was damaged and might come tumbling down if anything was disturbed. What was really frightening were the rats scurrying from nowhere and disappearing so fast. Added to the excitement was the fact that parents would be very angry if they got news from neighbours or passers-by of the "adventure".

HY: Again, fear and relief, fear and relief on avoiding danger. Do you have other early memories?

JZ: I do remember being about four years old. The war had ended but food, coal and household supplies were still rationed or limited. My father's employment came to an end and I remember the fearful atmosphere he brought into the house to explain to my mother that he was out of work. My parents, in their forties, were suddenly without income. I felt the anxiety in my father when each day he returned, tired and unhappy, having been out unsuccessfully looking for work. My mother had tried to explain to me what was happening, but I was too young to understand. The feeling of fear and anxiety, however, were very real to me. Then one day, after probably not very long, a school friend of my father, one of three brothers who were in business together, heard that my father was looking for work, came to the house and asked him to be manager of their company. There was a dramatic change of atmosphere in the house as my parents relaxed. I realised much later that these early memories were serious determinants for me; I had begun to fear living with fear, the seemingly irrational ups and downs of feeling, the emotional instability. Being an only child meant that there was no one with whom to compare notes.

It was then later, having met Don & Eugene that I learned to discuss, expose and neutralize the effects of such fears. When I first played guitar for Eugene I was so nervous, desperate for approval and its consequent emotional equilibrium. Eugene explained gently that the fears would diminish if I were to concentrate more on actually playing music and be less concerned with trying to impress others. There was a lot of work to be done together in many sessions before I could, in my skin, absorb what he had said and cease to be so badly affected by fear. The tyranny of it was eventually broken much later when I became annoyed with myself for suffering it yet again and suddenly saw clearly the futility of continuing to live in such a way.

Although there remain soft memory imprints they serve as useful references, and I thank Eugene for his time and patience spent in helping me to understand somewhat the nature of fear and its negative effect.

Hofner Senator Guitar

A model which John Zaradin was playing when he first met Eugene Halliday.

Personal Journey

Chapter 4
Defining Terms

I will say this only one more time, after which my lips are sealed:

It might be easier for a camel to go through the eye of a needle than for a rich person to enter the kingdom of heaven; it would all depend on how big the needle is, so don't get the hump.

Personal Journey

The Trap of Words

"Nearly all words learned since childhood are received from the commune emotionally charged and without adequate etymological definitions. To break out of this word-trapped state, one must study word origins, prime roots and affixes, and then readjust one's emotive reactions to the words. Words are power-forms, energies that work in communally determined ways until they are restored to their non-emotive, true significances".

Eugene Halliday. Contributions from a Potential Corpse II. Page 79

Deciding how one (and many others) should think

Académie Française defining terms in their own terms before their own term times have come.

HY: I would like to say that, in this kind of work, there are many questions and answers. We could remind ourselves here that an infant does not usually have a conscious vocabulary to define early events in its life, and that those events can become problematic because they are experienced emotionally and are relatively undefined. It is later that a person acquires a conscious vocabulary and is then able to research early memories and come to terms with them.

Eugene placed great emphasis on words and defining them.

JZ: He repeatedly proposed defining and creating an understanding of every word used.

He spoke of the emotional colour attached to a word and suggested that that also be examined. In fact, this was the essence of the engram work that we did together: re-live a memory, and in doing so, re-define the misunderstood 'trigger' words, unlocking thereby constrained pre-determined feelings; finally review and freely reassess the memory.

Because of those sessions, I started to build a 'phonic roots' language dictionary, grouping words by their root sources and sounds rather than by idea or concept. A simple routine with a new or unknown word would be to look at the way it is generally used; look at its etymology; then examine its sound and how physically it is produced; finally create a personal definition. It is quite remarkable how languages reduce themselves into each other when studied in this way.

HY: I understand that your studies at school were, in the main, with languages.

JZ: Yes. Don Lord was a great linguist and we had language as a shared interest. He encouraged me to study the different languages that I came across while traveling.

With hindsight, I was fascinated by the structures and grammar rather than the literature written in those languages. My interest was in how language worked as a system of communication. There is a kind of communication with oneself when working to find a suitable definition of a word, which makes it a useful activity when traveling alone. I am sure that there is no need to say that a little discretion is needed with this when in public places.

It is exciting, in using a language, to be able to communicate with another person, to make oneself understood with newly learned words and sounds. I loved to feel the nuances when attempting to express an idea from a new perspective or with different voices or accents, and then feeling a rapport with the person with whom I was trying to talk.

HY: This is, in fact, what an actor does all the time.

JZ: I agree. Even a little knowledge of language is such an asset when traveling and meeting new people.

The grouping of languages by sound, rather than sense, in effect, reduces the number of languages to study.

In fact, communication is much more direct without the constriction of trying to conceive distinct national languages. To create sounds for relation with other beings is a natural process for humans. It is possible to focus on the significance of vocal sounds and to consider the subtleties of the modalities of them, rather than to force a conception onto a sound or sounds. This locks the mind and can stop further thinking because the 'learned' meaning is accepted as already known.

HY: Could you give an example of what you mean?

JZ: Grouping the Romance languages into root sounds reduces the number of separate words to learn and opens a door with French and Italian, for example, to Greek through Latin, and with Spanish and Portuguese one is lead into Arabic.

When comparing the different common words for the same object or idea, local history and geography come into the picture. Spanish and Portuguese might use roots from Arabia and North Africa, but French, Italian and Romanian from Latin and Greek. History shows one movement of a culture around the southern coasts of the

Mediterranean and another around the northern coasts.

A simple example is the word olive, which arrives into French, Italian and Romanian from Greek and Latin but is not used in Spain and Portugal where the Arabic root zeitun, (aceituna) is used instead.

HY: It is a very interesting exercise to look at the origins of common words. The etymology of a word, where it appears in the world and when, can give a truer history of life than personal commentary.

JZ: Eugene might suggest: to analyze a word and its source, to look at the energy needed to physically produce its sound, to feel the emotion which accompanies the sound and, finally, to apply to that sound the understanding realised in the process.

HY: It sounds like a culinary recipe.

JZ: It is certainly food for thought.

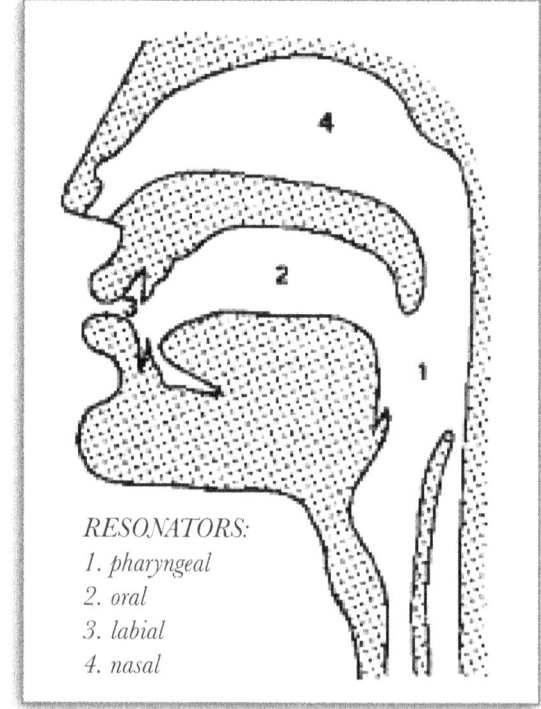

The speech organs

RESONATORS:
1. pharyngeal
2. oral
3. labial
4. nasal

The diagram was made by Eugene Halliday to prepare students for voice production and singing:

Effective breathing for speaking and singing is from the diaphragm and the lower ribs. In breathing in, the diaphragm should go down and the lower ribs should expand

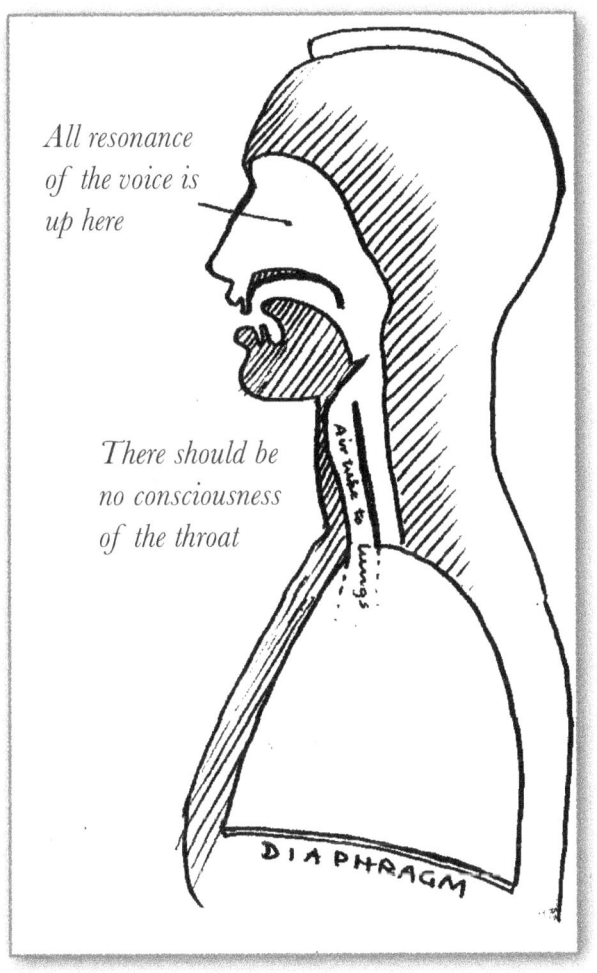

The diaphragm should be held down in vocalising.

The diaphragm is the 'platform' of the breath.

Personal Journey

Chapter 5

The Guitar

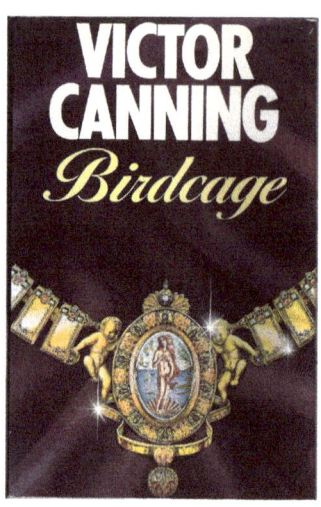

Herman laughed.

"There's not a fortune or a diagnosis that makes a sound like a guitar. Listen to that——"

he nodded at the tape recorder which he had brought from the garden with him and which was still playing.

"That's Zaradin. Every note is golden."

Victor Canning, Birdcage

"Each celestial body, in fact each and every atom, produces a particular sound on account of its movement, its rhythm or vibration. All these sounds and vibrations form a universal harmony in which each element, while having it's own function and character, contributes to the whole."

Pythagoras (569-475 BC)

Personal Journey

Kompakt Classical Guitar by Stephan Schlemper

HY: Next, how did you come to the guitar?

JZ: I was asked, at school, if I would like to play guitar in a group being formed and I said that I would. My parents were hesitant about spending money on a guitar until they knew that I could be serious about studying it. Having explained this to the trumpet playing organizer of the group, he lent me a cornet to practice on. I took it home and blew it loudly (how else?). My parents decided that a classical guitar might be a good idea after all and bought me a guitar but insisted that I take lessons.

HY: How did you feel about it?

JZ: I loved it, its shape and sound. I nursed it like a pet animal. Remember that it has a long history in its various forms; it now is involved in every field of music at all levels of complexity; it is portable, intimate and friendly. It requires thinking about to arrange fingerings to make music playable. It is emotionally very expressive in a variety of ways; it is a very physical instrument and requires muscle and stamina to play.

HY: What did it mean to you to begin to play the guitar?

JZ: It meant that I had found something of personal interest which gave me stability. It gave me confidence to be able to offer an opinion; I could accept another's viewpoint on a musical issue but felt that mine was equally valid. This is not a case of better or worse but equally valid accepting different viewpoints. I remember that there was a moment, at the beginning, when I was trying to play a simple study and suddenly something in the sound of the guitar told me how the study should be played; I was simply in a feeling mood that had taken me over and in which I knew what to do. I sensed a world to which I could relate and that world was mine to explore.

I discovered a personal security hidden in the manipulation of a few pieces of wood which someone had put together as a guitar.

I had found something to which I could give myself.

From then on I was committed to relating to the world as a guitar player, as "He who plays the guitar." As a teenager it was very annoying and frustrating that whenever I left the house with the guitar, people would notice and say "Look, a singer." "He has a guitar he must be a singer." "Sing us a song." I was often asked "What do you sing?" There seemed to be no one, apart from my teachers, asking me to *play* the instrument, no one who saw the guitar itself as a means of expression. The perception of the man in the street, seeing me with my guitar, was that it was an instrument only played to accompany the voice. As far as I knew, pianists and violinists did not suffer this. These players were assumed to play, to be instrumentalists. Worse, with the popularity of rock and roll, the guitar was seen as steel strung or electric and used only to accompany popular songs. It undermined my own image of myself that I was seen to be a popular singer when I saw myself as a serious musician who could make sounds with a guitar which would change and heal the soul of anyone who heard it. I had no wish to be identified with any popular song movement and I did my best when carrying a guitar in public to hide it. Even now I do that, my guitar cases are made to be unobtrusive, unnoticeable. I wished others to know me by the music that I played, not by their misconceptions of what they thought me to be. I wished personal relationships with music not general crowd associations. I wished to be unseen unless it was time to be a guitarist, when I could then relate to others through a persona that I felt to be the reality of me.

Is all this the egotism of an only child, fantasy of a teenager? I was furious that no one seemed to relate to me as a guitarist, but as a singer. I even refused to be able to sing, even when it would have been helpful and later very useful. My voice had to be the sound of the guitar.

This commitment became, more and more, a serious determinant and problematic in relations with others until I met Don Lord and Eugene. Eugene in particular showed that he valued the guitar as a means of expression as much as I did (maybe there is a clue here to his character) and I was overcome at finding someone in the world who understood how I felt about the instrument.

I can now see that my whole life from this time was turning in such a way that it had value only if others related to me as a classical guitar player. I was seeing that if my place in the world was not as a guitarist then it was nothing, and this I came to believe. The problem is that at essential level this is not a true perception: being a guitar player is a role played by the will to discover its own potentialities which, when fulfilled, must re-conceive itself and finally know that it is no mere conception but the creator of conceptions. I saw that to *identify* is to *feign to die* and it seemed that all the trials and tribulations, the silly fears, the nervousness, the negativity through life were self-imposed and, if seen to have any purpose, that purpose is to show that they have no purpose other than to prove the will to itself and release it from its *feign to die* or *identify*-cation.

There were so many years of fearfully presenting myself as a serious being worthy of the attention of intelligent people; there was careless non-attention to others who seemed not to know how to be serious with themselves. I wished to prove to the world that, with a few pieces of wood, I was sage, king and pauper with a kaleidoscope of expression in one organism. For me, the guitar has been instrumental in opening up a way of life and, with each new experience presented, has been an uncompromising constant, continually obliging me to ask myself what I was doing. Finally, it exhausted its carrier body possibilities and, in becoming dust, allowed a will to see itself free and able to continue anew.

This is what it has meant to me to play the guitar.

HY: Tell us more about the guitar.

JZ: What I did not immediately appreciate was the fact that the guitar was not a traditional mainstream instrument. Its concert stage repertoire, compared with that of the violin and piano, was small. It could produce little volume and its nuances of sound and colour were lost if it combined to play with other instruments. The traditional musical establishments at the time considered it as a secondary instrument reserved for special effects, novelty items and folk music. Eugene saw it as a very expressive instrument that in various forms had been played over a long period of time; there is a biblical reference to a guitar during the Hittite period some 3,600 years ago, and it is still with us today. I felt that I could commit my life to the guitar and Eugene gave full support to this. Andrés Segovia had brought it to the concert platform and was inspiring composers to create new repertoire. Since the 1950s it has been evolving in many directions with guitar makers greatly improving its construction. A positive aspect of the electric guitar has been the financial investment into the 'business' of the guitar. Its popularity has enabled companies to produce extremely well made and professionally useable guitars and has also inspired into being new generations of individual guitar makers. In this computer age, it can even be used as a Musical Instrument Digital Interface (acronym MIDI) and, like the piano and keyboards, trigger the sound libraries of other instruments to become in effect an orchestra simulating strings, wind and percussion. Microphone and sound studio advances have given the classical guitar its own niche in recorded music. Rebalancing of sound electronically has allowed orchestral music to be written for it; it can now be scored to play with other instruments and be featured and *heard*; this alone has expanded the techniques needed to play the instrument and has created musical opportunities for the player that did not exist when I first met Eugene.

Personal Journey

SoloEtte Travel Guitar by Wright Guitar Technology

Within the 'body' is a small cavity with a pair of stereo microphones. The metal frames detach for traveling.

Close-up of an interesting guitar at the Frankfurt Musikmesse.

Guitarist Vernon Fischer of Virginia declares "Of course it goes in the overheads, it goes right over my head." I do not know whether a hard case or soft would be better, but I shall need both footstool and sling.

Author's Note:

It is written that the original of this guitar was made for Goliath, the famous Gittite player of Gath. Biblical references to Goliath's being stoned as a result of his association with the celebrated song-writer and lyrical lyricist, David, are disputed, and contemporary consensus is that his condition was caused by the fact that, "at four cubits and a span", he stood, like Saul, a good "head taller than anyone else in all Israel" and was thereby inspired by the rarified air that he continuously breathed.

Editor's Note: content for this note is unverified.

Personal Journey

Godin Multiac

A MIDI interface guitar which serves as a computer controller and played by John Zaradin on several recordings.

*André Segovia
Original sketch by
Theresa McAllister.*

Details of the concert programme on which was created the above sketch.

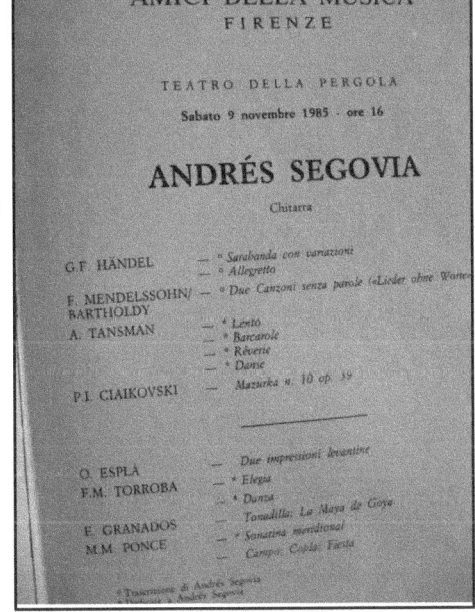

Personal Journey

Chapter 6
Tuition in Music

Pitch range of the guitar showing where each note is found on the fingerboard

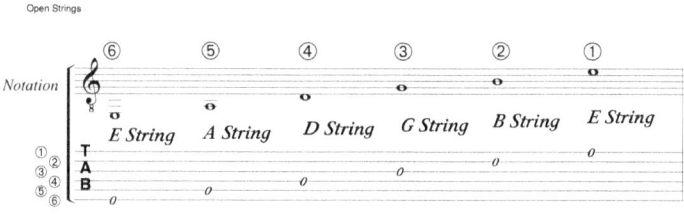

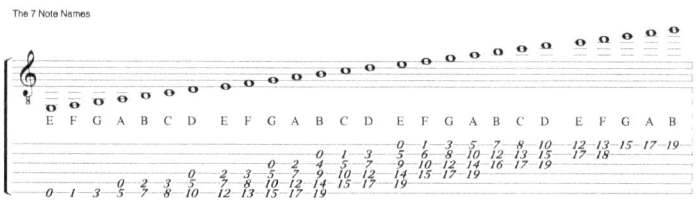

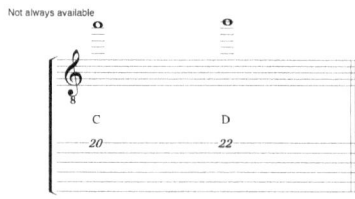

Personal Journey

J.S. Bach *once offered an organ student some remarkably simple advice: Organ playing he said, "...is nothing remarkable..., all one has to do is hit the right notes at the right time and the instrument plays itself."*

"I was obliged to be industrious. Whoever is equally industrious will succeed . . . equally well."

"If I decide to be an idiot, then I'll be an idiot on my own accord."

HY: Next, to your music teachers.

JZ: My first teacher, an Asian Indian, taught me the basics of classical guitar. His approach and encouragement inspired me to play and I looked forward to the weekly lessons.

Interestingly, one of the first things that he did at the beginning of each lesson was to massage the body of the guitar in order to warm up the wood and integrate the sound, exactly as a body masseur would do. Eugene did the same with my guitars later; he would hold and stroke them and I always felt that they had become better instruments because of it.

HY: Positive nervous energy again.

JZ: I can see now, years later, that when my fingers produced some sounds and patterns from that guitar I was changed forever. I had a new feeling that I had not experienced with anything else. Understand that it is later looking back that I see how I was; at the time I just felt well with the instrument.

HY: Looking at a general picture, we could say that, with your first teacher, you had found on the inside a will to something, something to which you could apply yourself.

JZ: My second teacher was a piano player, doubling guitar, who taught me how to read at sight, improvise and play in ensembles. He worked hard to turn me away from the idea of becoming a professional musician and pressed me to qualify at school with educational subjects separate from music. He explained that as one gets older life can become difficult for a performing musician, especially a guitar player. He meant well, reflecting on his own position, but the more he talked to me the more determined I became to succeed as a guitar player.

HY: With him however, you studied general performing techniques which included ensemble playing. You began to learn how to apply your energy and your skills. The advice of your teacher, although appearing to be negative, was actually increasing your determination to be involved with music. The pressure of his advice was creating in you a self-determination.

JZ: The contradictions caused by so much well-meaning advice compounded the problems of puberty and I started to fall to pieces. I can say that I gained an idea of what it feels like to be in the process of disintegration, to be dying by dissipation and watching oneself daily becoming more vague, evaporating into the nothing, the *néant*, the void. I began to stammer, lost confidence, became very clumsy and then fell over tearing the ligaments in my left knee. This brought me, in every way, to a full stop as I could not walk properly. In the middle of this was the persistent feeling that I wanted to be a musician or nothing at all. After all, there were professional guitar players in the world, not many, but they did exist and I wanted to be one of them. There seemed to be nothing worth pursuing if not music (all this without having any idea of how the business of music functioned).

HY: I understand that when your second teacher became ill and could no longer teach, he recommended that you continue your studies with a pianist who was both player and teacher of music theory. Why would he recommend you to a pianist?

JZ: Because there was no other local guitar teacher.

However, this third teacher was for me, fantastic. He taught me so much; the lessons were on Sundays and lasted all afternoon or until his wife appeared to remind him that he had to prepare himself to play in the evening.

I learned from him that music was not a detached activity, but was something the whole world related to in one way or another. I saw with him that being a professional musician was a reality.

He was very interested in mysticism and philosophy, encompassing freemasonry, Rosicrucianism, spiritualism etc. We looked at the recorded activities of Madame Blavatsky, Aleister Crowley and then musicians such as Cyril Scott, Scriabin and Arnold Bax. There was a focus on what he called the mathematical basis of the arts, combining music, dance, architecture, painting and literature into one study.

This teacher, pianist Albert Kay, was one of the seven certified teachers of the "Schillinger System of Musical Composition" and he had students from all fields of music. He set up correspondence courses in the UK and internationally for those not living close enough to visit him. Roy Castle, trumpet player, comedian and actor was a pupil of his at that time.

HY: How old were you then?

JZ: About fifteen or sixteen years. I continued with him until I was nineteen, by which time I had met Don and Eugene, who suggested that I obtain a scholarship for music school. Albert agreed that it was a very good idea and helped me prepare for the audition, which proved to be successful, and finally set me off in a direction that I felt was of my own choosing.

HY: With your third teacher we could say that you learned to analyze and understand the structures of music and he prepared you for working with other musicians.

JZ: Yes, the tuition dealt with all elements and techniques of practical music making.

HY: Let us now introduce Eugene Halliday as a teacher and understand that he did not at all focus on the mechanics *per se* but on the relationship of the musician himself with the mechanics. He stated that the musician needs to continually balance and rebalance mind and body as the music is played and heard. He taught that there was a direct relationship between the conscious live energy and the form of the persona by means of which the music is sounded.

JZ: A good teacher does not tell his pupil how to play; he instructs the pupil in such a way that the pupil learns how to do so by uncovering and discovering for himself his own way of playing. There were times when I wished Eugene would tell me how to play something, but he never did, because that would have created, as I later understood, a dependency on him. He always worked in such a way that the solution of a problem appeared within me. The lessons were always in terms of self-control and feeling into the music to let it play itself; this meant *let it play* because it will play, as I would wish, if I let it do it. He was ever so careful not to interfere with the growth of the pupil who was always directed to feel inside himself and look for his own individual contribution.

It can be very difficult for a good teacher—being able to help but restraining himself from doing so in order to let the talents of the pupil develop naturally and at their own pace.

-♃ ♄ ☿-

"Latin" is not a dead language.

Leslie Booth and Ian Sands join John Zaradin for a "Latin" evening at the Sondaur Music Club.

Chapter 7
Joseph Schillinger

"What makes us feel drawn to music is that our whole being is music: our mind and body, the nature in which we live, the nature which has made us, all that is beneath and around us, it is all music."

Hazrat Inyat Khan (Sufi Master) (1882-1927)

Joseph Schillinger (1895 - 1943) was born in Kharkov, Ukraine (at that time, part of Russia). He was an exceptional student throughout this academic life and graduated from the Classical College in 1914 and the St. Petersburg Imperial Conservatory of Music.

He arrived in the United States of America in 1928 and received his citizenship in 1936. He remained there until his death in 1943 at the age of 47. In his short life Joseph Schillinger achieved a great deal in the area of music and composition theory. He was a music teacher at Columbia Teachers College and also gave private lessons at his home with George Gershwin, Glenn Miller, Carmine Coppola ("Godfather" films and father of film director Francis Ford Coppola) numbering amongst his pupils. During this time he developed his ideas which became published as the "Schillinger System of Musical Composition" by Joseph Schillinger, compiled by Lyle Dowling and Arnold Shaw. The work was published posthumously and is still deemed incomplete by his original students. One of his students, Lawrence Berk, founded the Schillinger House of Music, later to be named the Berklee College of Music at Boston, Massachusetts, USA.

It is not clear how many teachers Schillinger himself certified for his system. The number is believed to be between seven and twelve with only seven substantiated.

Personal Journey

Joseph Schillinger

Berklee College of Music

In 1945 pianist, composer, arranger and MIT graduate Lawrence Berk founded Schillinger House, the precursor to the Berklee School of Music. He felt that students should study with players rather than academics, and in the main hired working musicians as faculty members.

The school specialized in the Schillinger System of harmony and composition developed by Joseph Schillinger, who had been Berk's teacher. At the time of its founding almost all music schools focused primarily on classical music, but Schillinger House offered training in jazz and commercial music for radio, theatre, television, and dancing. When it opened, most of the students were working professional musicians.

It is now the largest independent college of contemporary music in the world and has become the world's foremost institute for the study of jazz and modern American music. The curriculum, however, includes all fields of music. In 1945 there were some 40 students. Today there are over 4,000.

HY: So far, we have seen how early memories can establish themselves as hidden roots of character growth and become the unconscious causes of one's reactions, both positively and negatively, in daily life.

We have seen a genuine interest arise through music, which caused you to apply your energies to studying how to play the guitar and then to understanding the structures of music, your chosen subject. What happened next?

JZ: With this arose a will to overcome externally imposed inertias of education and environmental conditioning (read here anyone trying to tell me what I should be doing), which had been mainly until I met Eugene (and Don), negative. Being with Eugene allowed me to envisage a persona through which, on my own terms, I might be able to relate to the rest of the world.

HY: In the third stage of your music education you mention Joseph Schillinger. Who was he?

JZ: Joseph Schillinger was the first composer to write for the theremin, an early electronic instrument controlled without physical contact and triggered by moving your hand or even your body into its energy field to modulate the sound. It was invented by the Russian Leon Theremin, who patented it in 1928. The theme music for the UK TV series "Midsomer Murders" is played on the theremin, and it is often heard in "ghost" movies.

Schillinger was a Russian émigré to the USA who died in the year 1943, which was the year I was born. He formulated the "Schillinger System of Musical Composition" and a second complementary work entitled "Mathematical Basis of the Arts", in which the underlying structures of music, sculpture, painting, architecture and so on, are studied, analyzed and compared. Often with music studies attention is directed towards idiom, style and associated techniques for playing. Schillinger stressed the study of basic structures to which idiom and style would be applied as required.

HY: That is rather like looking at life through Eugene's window of thinking, feeling and willing.

So what exactly is the "Schillinger System of Musical Composition"?

JZ: It is a set of tools with which to analyze music into its fundamental components. It begins with a theory of rhythm, on which are based subsequent theories of melody, harmony, counterpoint, form and semantics.

HY: What are these tools?

JZ: Exercises and studies, which open up ways of manipulating the above components, and which lead to an understanding of them as mathematical patterns evident everywhere in nature.

The first theory is that of rhythm, which underlies the whole treatise, and must be fully understood before the remaining theories can be studied because these evolve out of the principles proposed in the rhythm theory.

HY: Eugene has defined music as the "physical structure of reality".

JZ: By this he is saying that the alternating compression and decompression, the breathing and pulsing, which creates sound, is life itself living. The Artist, Musician, Composer is sensitive to the field modulations and, by will, selects patterns for sound expression. Bach, for example, is said to be a universal musician because he is sensitive to harmonizing universal structures; he realised those patterns with his music. If you hear and give yourself to that music you feel your whole organism unifying itself and becoming healthier and liberated as you breathe the physical vibrations of the sounds.

HY: Therefore music is not an analogy of life, it is that very life, living and breathing.

JZ: Schillinger supports this by beginning his treatise with the idea of a simple compression and release of energy, that is a movement in the field, which, when activated by an instrument, such as a drum, produces a one-beat noise or note.

HY: That reminds me of the way Eugene used to illustrate the beginning of creation through compaction of energy, by making a dot on a white sheet of paper. The white paper was the original, unmodified, universal sentient power source.

JZ: Repeat that same frequency of compression and release to hear a series of mono sounding beats; a drum beat is an example of such.

HY: Then he would show how a repeated pattern of dots or compressions could appear as a line.

JZ: When time varies between the attacks we perceive the time value differences and conceive rhythm.

HY: Eugene's line would begin to wander and form wave patterns, looping over its own pathway to create whirlpools of energy, particles, beings, or, in this case, sounds.

JZ: If the frequency changes we hear notes sounding higher and lower in space and can conceive of them as a scale or melody.

HY: From this I understand that the horizontal length of time between the attacks—the periodicities—gives us rhythm. The vertical difference in space between the frequencies—the speed or rate of compression-release of the field producing the notes—gives us pitch. Together, they give us melody.

JZ: Not to forget that a frequency, which we hear as a pitch or note, is only differentiated from what we perceive as a rhythm, by its speed; that is, how much time is needed to compress and decompress the medium.

HY: Yes, and, as Eugene always reminded us: the medium or matter, is a form of energy, not a separate substance.

JZ: A simple everyday example is a police or ambulance siren; if it approaches you, the rate or speed of the pressure-release increases and the frequency of the sound rises; but if it goes away from you, the pressure-release decreases and the frequency of the sound goes down.

If it becomes slow enough the siren noise is heard, not as a siren, but as separate pulses, not as a continuous sound, but as a rhythm.

Imagine walking beside a metal railing dragging a stick along it: you hear separate distinct clicks. Now imagine running faster so that, with the faster compression and release, the clicks start to merge into a note or sound.

In the same way visually, we accept film and TV pictures as continuous, but we know that the apparent continuity is a fast presentation of separate picture frames.

Similarly, a guitar is a 'tune' instrument because it can produce note frequencies fast enough to give the effect of continuity. There is a faster repetition of the compression and release of energy than with a metal railing.

The physical structure of the instrument permits the interference and summing of different rates of compression and release and produces the individual sounds and colours of each instrument.

Rhythm and pitch are different speeds of one and the same energy field compressing and releasing itself with expression by the medium of a musical instrument.

HY: Come home Einstein, all is forgiven. We are on home territory with Eugene and Space Time Power.

Schillinger explained music as mathematics.

JZ: They both saw the mathematics in music and the music in mathematics and thereby were sensing a holistic world.

HY: How was this integration of all functions mathematically presented to you?

JZ: A basic model for envisaging music is a graph paper grid, conceiving space, up and down and time, left to right along it.

For pitch: create a zero axis point on the grid and give that point a pitch reference; it can be the note of the key of the piece (C, Bb and so on).

Decide on values for the grid units.

In the traditional music system one square up or down on the grid equals a step of one semitone; two steps a tone and so on. If the music is in the key of C then two steps up would be the note D. Two steps down would be the note Bb (A#).

For time: a one square move along the grid equals a predetermined time value which is in practice the shortest, that is fastest, note unit in the piece which is usually 8th, 16th, 32nd or 64th note, or even a real time value such as a second)

When a melody is plotted, its contour in time and space can been seen clearly. Its construction is easily appreciated.

Wolfgang Amadeus Mozart 1756-1791

The Order of the Golden Spur was presented to Mozart in 1770.

Personal Journey

The graph below is an example of the above, showing a four measure extract of the melody trajectory of Mozart's "Rondo Alla Turka"

Reading up ↑ and down ↓ gives pitch values;

Reading along → gives time values.

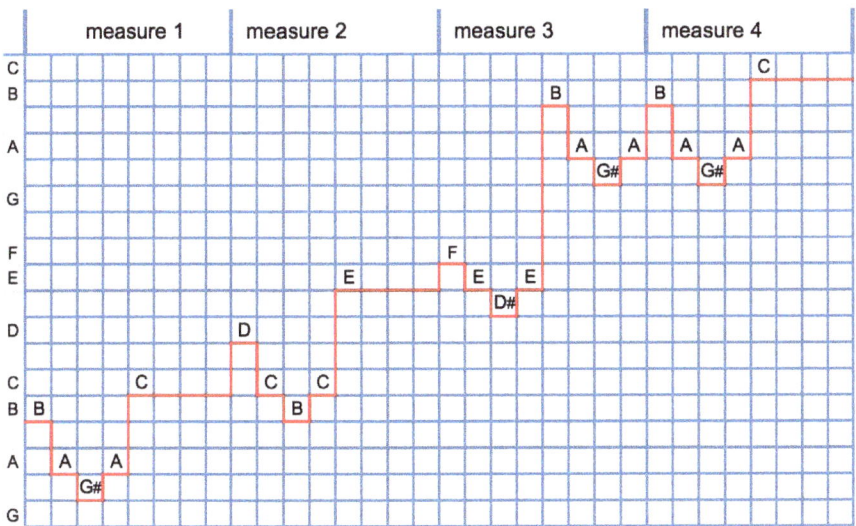

HY: So when you understood the graphics as music you began to understand mathematics.

JZ: The contours of good music can be used as templates on which new music, in other styles, can be written, and this music will sound "correct".

Schillinger stated that his theories, exercises and studies were to serve as guides for the composer and arranger. He emphasized that the musician would still need to feel for his own music patterns, his own music, but he would do it more efficiently if he were trained to identify and understand the elements involved.

HY: Could you give an example of an exercise or study?

JZ: A dramatic or emotional scenario would be set and the student was required to compose suitable music.

An example could be a film sequence, where a door handle in semi darkness turns, the door opens a little allowing sight of an indistinct moving shadow in the adjacent room: what music can you imagine?

HY: Interesting. You are instructed to interpret a situation, feel its emotion and then create suitable music.

JZ: Exactly. One exercise was to find music underscoring a street scene where a mother and child are playing with a balloon. The balloon floats high into the air and the mother and child start to run following its direction; the camera pans into the air with the balloon and watches it burst against a telephone cable. The noise of the balloon bursting is simultaneous with the noise of a car crashing and someone (off camera) screams.

The brief is to write x number of seconds of music for that scene.

HY: You were studying this after school?

JZ: Yes, and it helped me at school. At home after each lesson I would try to conceive music for a scenario and also copy out and arrange the exercises so that they could be played on the guitar.

I used to listen to the rhythms produced by surrounding noise. For example, on a train there was always a *daga da da daga da da* from the wheels on the track which changed when the train, arriving at a station, slowed down (making musically, a *rallentando*) and accelerated (making musically, an *accellerando*) on leaving. Even people in a bar or café create multiple rhythms when they are all speaking differently but in the same room and at the same time. I was enthused to convert what I was hearing into music language.

Later when Eugene talked about Space Time Power there was a link to my music lessons. He would be referencing space up and down and times along on the axes. Space as melody, because it is taking up space, and Time because it is creating movement. The new consideration for me, added by Eugene, was the dynamic element of Power; how much energy is involved with the referenced Space and Time.

HY: You were learning musical composition and theory without playing the piano. This meant that you transcribed for the guitar what was explained to you on the piano.

JZ: Yes, I started with the guitar at the age of thirteen and at about sixteen, because of my particular teachers, my studies were directed more to music theory. The guitar took centre stage again when I gained the scholarship at nineteen.

My music education was therefore hybrid. However, as a teenager, being able to cross-reference different art forms, approach the avant-garde, esoteric philosophies and mysticism, was invigorating.

At this time many musicians were experimenting with sound and colour, doubling up the note frequencies into the visual colour spectrum and looking at the mathematical relationships between the different elements. Scriabin was such a composer.

A Russian exhibition at Earl's Court, London, dedicated rooms to synchronizing light and sound. Light colours were triggered by the music with the strength of the attack on a note changing the intensity of the colour.

HY: This is now everyday disco.

JZ: And so it is.

When I started to attend the talks of Eugene, at Ishval, I could relate, through melody, rhythm and dynamics, to the concepts of Space Time Power that he presented.

Personal Journey

A graph of the first four measures of the melody of "Easter Song" by Eugene Halliday.

Reading up ↑ and down ↓ gives pitch values.

Reading along → gives time values.

A graph of the first four measure

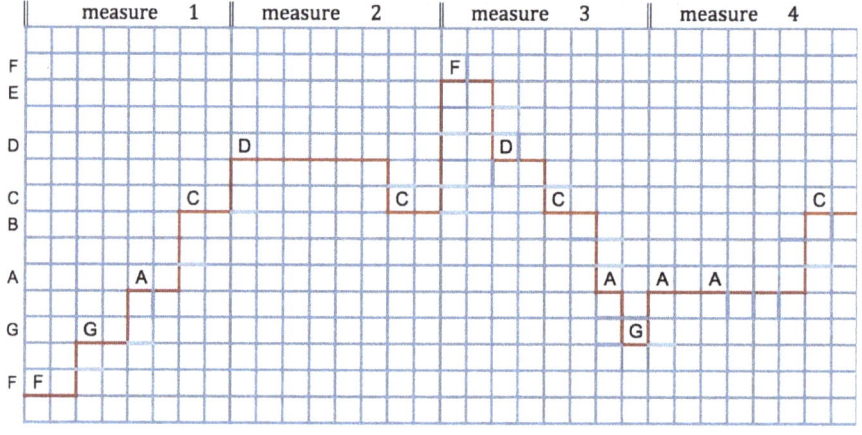

The above graph in music notation

Personal Journey

All aspects of music playing and production - instruments, recording equipment, publishing, lighting and accessories - are presented annually at music fairs around the world; one of the largest is at Frankfurt Musikmesse in Germany

On the stand at the Frankfurt Musikmesse

The Mel Bay Publications team "get into" a guitar tutorial.

A guitar quartet class at Chemin de Guitardou

The audience could relate the four elements of Fire, Earth, Air and Water as life energy sounding itself through four guitars playing musical forms infused with feeling.

Guitar Quartet at Chemin de Guitardou

Eric Hill, John Zaradin, Peter Stanley and Peter Barratt.

Personal Journey

Chapter 8

Musical Space Time Power

"*He that divines the secret of my music is freed from the unhappiness that haunts the whole world of men.*"

"*Music is the mediator between the life of the senses and the life of the spirit.*"

Beethoven (1770-1827)

"*Pythagoras based musical education in the first place on certain melodies and rhythms that exercised a healing, a purifying influence on the human actions and passions, restoring 'Pristine Harmony' of the soul's faculties. He applied the same means to the curing of diseases of both body and mind…*"

Porphyry (233-309)

2nd generation disciple of Pythagoras

"*The wonders of the music of the future will be of a higher & wider scale and will introduce many sounds that the human ear is now incapable of hearing. Among these new sounds will be the glorious music of angelic chorales. As men hear these they will cease to consider Angels as figments of their imagination.*"

Mozart (1756-1791)

Personal Journey

God walking in the garden by Eugene Halliday. (Scraperboard c. 1950)

HY: I see the ideas of Space and Time but what was taught vis à vis Power, Dynamics?

JZ: Technically, one would consider, at any given moment, the number of instruments playing, and the level of sound required for the music, that is how soft, how loud. Next, one could look to establish a mood or emotional effect by the type of instrument playing. Wind, strings and percussion all have their own basic colours and qualities: bowed strings can sustain a sound indefinitely, wind instruments can sustain for a limited time, percussive instruments call your attention to the note at the moment of attack. Dynamics are created by contrasting or blending these elements with greater or lesser degrees of expectancy.

If the basic idea for the music is a particular mood then dynamics can be created in the rhythm or in key or tonal centre changes. If the rhythm is the focus, the introduction of volume changes or different sound colours will add interest. If a melody is the centre of attention, supporting it with different note clusters, or chords, will create different tensions as it progresses.

When you become familiar with those fundamental components and can hear and feel them, you notice that the composers that you tend to listen to repeatedly do not actually make exact repeats of patterns; there are always subtle changes and by these the music is always interesting, especially so with a performer sensitive to those nuances. It is rather like breathing, where there is a slightly different dynamic with each breath. If the absolute notes, frequencies, stay the same then you do something different with the dynamic, with the power of it, and then with the timing of it.

HY: I can relate the music of Mozart to this—his interrupted cadences. I love him because he actually reveals fundamental, organic structures of life.

JZ: It was very exciting to discover the technicalities of music and to learn that there were principles involved that could be studied and applied. There is a danger, however, of ignoring spontaneity and relying only on what you *know*, because the application of the techniques permits a mechanical writing that works structurally and produces acceptable music. Today, radio and television are filled with repetitive computer generated emotionally empty sounds which are put together using principles that are legitimate and *sound*.

To be so trained showed itself to be a problem when I met Don and Eugene; I was so conditioned by sets of rules that it was impossible to hear music trying to analyze it. It was impossible for me to play freely from myself because the training interfered. Eventually, it was Don who said that I should stop studying as I had been, and let my imposing education fall away so that I could breathe again and feel music without the filters which had built up from concentrated studying.

HY: This is not to say that the education in itself was incorrect but the way that you absorbed it was.

There were egotistical issues, which interfered.

JZ: The exercises and studies in the system equip you with a database of compositional ideas; clips of melodic styles, chord sounds and moods, an awareness of the semantics of music. This aspect is very useful especially when the composer has a brief to write, not what he imagines, but what a film or stage director would like for a particular scenario. The director may require a special music effect on a picture frame with a 30 second build into that frame; in this instance it is the end which is important, so the composer might write the music backwards from the end to the beginning, plotting his music along the time grid.

Technically, the music has, at a certain time, to coincide with a picture frame, so put that in first, and write the music backwards to the start point, be it many seconds, minutes or frames away.

Psychologically, this means that instead of starting off and going somewhere, the composer looks back from the point of arrival and uncovers a pathway to it.

Personal Journey

HY: What happens when the film is edited, if a scene is shortened or lengthened? Is the music cut or does the composer rewrite?

JZ: Before computers arrived, the composer needed to rewrite, but now music recording programs can scale the timings, meaning that the music can be stretched or compressed into more or less time without the composer having to do a rewrite.

HY: Do you compose music for the guitar or by means of it? That is, do you hear the music first and then arrange it for the instrument or do the ideas for music arise as you hold the guitar?

JZ: Both, but in fact, it is generally more interesting to sit with the guitar exploring and discovering new patterns.

Physically playing bypasses thinking and produces ideas much more interesting and individual than those worked out intellectually. Actively playing seems to produce ideas out of nowhere and surprise me. In fact there are some pieces published which, from myself, I would never have conceived and written but nonetheless have put together spontaneously.

Camera crossover "Be My Guest" with Elias Chalouhi

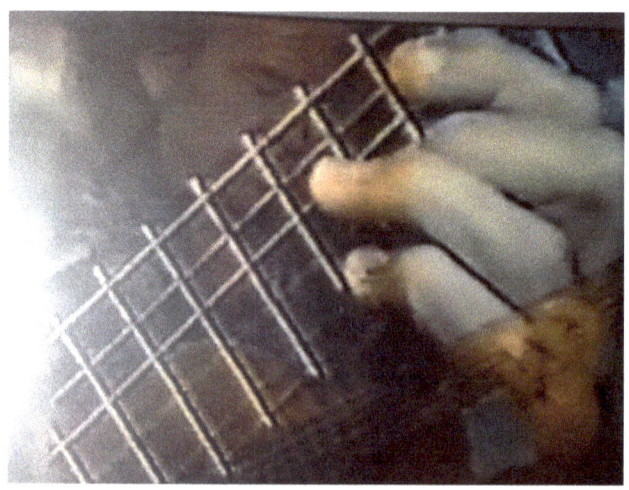

Live interview and performance on QatarTV, Doha.

The unseen face of the guitar

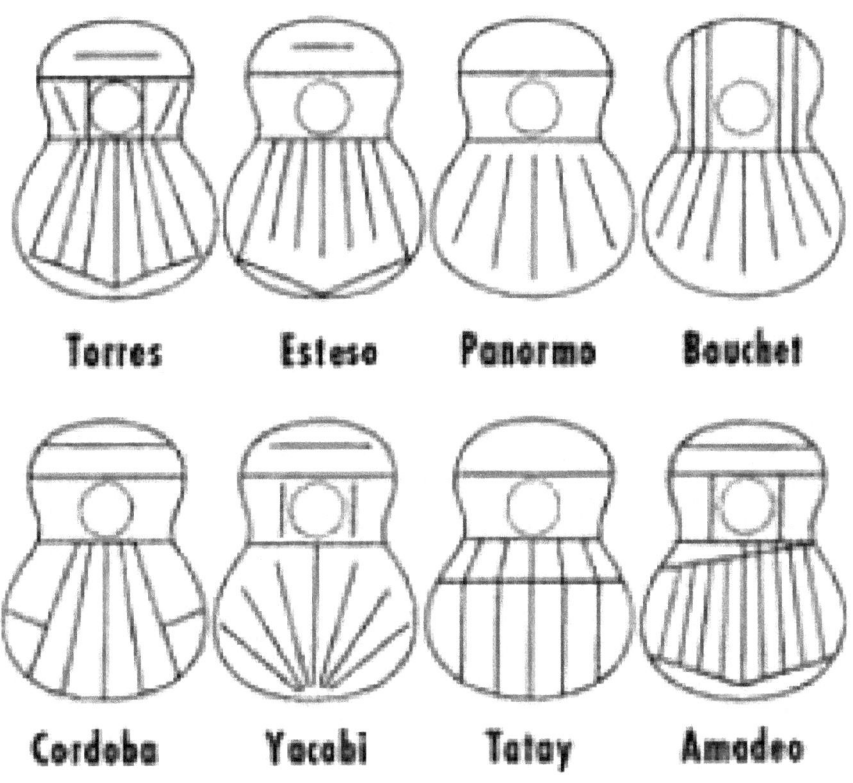

The varied positions of the "bracings" affect how the sound waves are distributed inside the instrument. Each of the eight patterns, created by the named makers, causes the wood of the guitar to vibrate in a unique way, affecting the tone colours that the instrument produces.

Personal Journey

Chapter 9

To Be Or Not To Be

(A Guitar Player)

About to depart for Dubai

Is all this really necessary?

Personal Journey

"It is a funny thing, but when I am making music, all the answers I seek for in life seem to be there, in the music.

Or rather, I should say, when I am making music, there are no questions and no need for answers."

Gustav Mahler (1860-1911)

John Zaradin's group Images of Brasil at Ronnie Scott's Jazz Club, London

"If I were not a physicist, I would probably be a musician. I often think in music. I live my daydreams in music. I see my life in terms of music."

Albert Einstein (1879-1955)

HY: You are now in your mid-teens and studying mainly music theory?

JZ: Yes. During this time a bout of bronchitis kept me in bed at home and gave me time to copy out the lessons which contained charts showing the logic of music, how notes relate to each other and combine to form new relations, how they function within particular scales and chords.

HY: With this you had begun to have an understanding of music and could play the guitar.

As you became more and more absorbed by your music studies how did you balance your school work?

JZ: I lost interest in all school activities except for the music lessons. The school music teacher suggested that I play two pieces in an end of term school concert. I prepared an arrangement of "*Malagueña*", by Ernesto Lecuona, and a piece entitled "*Tomorrow's Daydream*", by Ivor Mairants.

The teacher invited me to his house after school to work on the interpretations.

His instruction was expert and the concert, with the whole school in attendance, went very well. It was the first time that most of the audience had heard a guitar played live and the enthusiastic response and applause convinced me that life with a guitar was wonderful.

However, the experience did not help me with school studies as I became increasingly determined to have a life in music. The real problem was that there was no pre-set course for a classical guitar player, not even an academic one, as there was for piano and violin. In London there were opportunities for working as an electric guitar player—studio sessions, musicals, hotel work and functions, but all this was casual with no progressive route that anyone could see, there was no career.

HY: The problem was how to survive as a guitar player without being at least semi-professional?

JZ: There was a positive outcome from the concert when another music teacher at the school came to talk to me. Having agreed that the lower four strings of the guitar were tuned like the double bass and that I would, in principle, be able to read bass parts, he said he needed a bass player for a local Christmas show that he was conducting. He then gave me some parts and told me to look at them, adding that I should appear for rehearsals at a local, named theatre, at the time to be given, and where there would be a double bass waiting for me. Again all went well, and at the end of the show he handed me a tie as payment which I accepted happily with my blistered fingers and which I still keep as a memento. Although I was inexperienced and nervous, I enjoyed the challenge tremendously and felt an excitement and satisfaction from playing with other musicians that is very different from playing as a soloist.

HY: Right. I am sure that Eugene would have approved of your accepting such a challenge.

JZ: As a result I became increasingly involved with music, to the detriment of everything else. I started to listen to jazz and was intrigued by the improvising. In the early hours of the morning I searched on long wave radio for the Voice of America "Willis Connover Jazz Hour". At school I was asked to join a band that was being formed with violin, piano, bass and drums. We played school dances, Conservative and Labour club evenings and because we were paid (a little!) a vision of a perfect life started to form itself.

HY: And this is while you were still at school.

JZ: However, I really had lost interest there, and when my school days ended I burned everything except my French, German and Latin books. I wanted a completely fresh start. The contradiction between knowing what I wanted to do and trying to adjust to what other, well meaning, advisors were suggesting, caused me great distress. The accident, to which we referred earlier, tearing the ligaments in my left knee, did indeed, bring me to a halt and to a crossroads where I could hardly move for some six months. Although I could not easily move I could study music.

Albert Kay had given me so many exercises and ideas to work on. There were charts of voice leadings showing how notes related to each other and how their values changed as their functions changed. He insisted that I manually copy them out. He said that if I copied them and applied them to the guitar I would never need to refer to them again, but if I merely read them I would need to refer to them for the rest of my life. I took him at his word and started copying. After many hours of writing the logic behind the patterns suddenly became clear and I understood what he was trying to teach me. It really was like a light being switched on. I still have the charts, mainly to explain to others (if they should ask) how I was taught.

HY: Six months with your leg in plaster,

JZ: Yes, but not my hands, not my mind.

HY: Studying musical charts of voice leadings and chord structures. What are voice leadings and chord structures?

JZ: When a musician refers to voice leadings he is referring to a musical grammar. Music sounds 'correct' and balanced in its form when its structural ratios conform to this grammar or syntax. A voice leading is a function that infers the logic of the music when that music progresses in time from one note to another or from one chord to another. If we are sensitive to the grammar, the voice leading creates expectancy and we begin to feel that we *know* the music.

Linguistically, we can think of subject—verb—object:

subject *man*—verb *plays*—object *guitar*. *man* focuses attention; *plays* tells us he is doing something; *guitar* tells us what he is playing (doing).

A function relates one thing to another. Here the word *plays* functions as a voice leading, informing us of a relation between *man* and *guitar*.

The voice leading is a constant but its function changes with context. If we look at the two sentences: Man *has* guitar. Man *has* left (unstated: place). In the second sentence the function of *has* has changed. *Man has guitar* gives the idea of possession; *Man has left* gives the idea of action without any sense of possession. The function is created by that on which our attention is focused—at any given moment in time.

As an exercise:

- Focus only on the word *man* and look inside yourself for some significance.

- Focus only on the words *man has* and note your internal changes.

- Focus on the words *man has guitar* and note even more complex changes.

Listening to music is in parallel to this. Listen to how the sense of the music is modified by focusing and re-focusing of your attention. Listen to the whole orchestration as sound colour then select an instrument or instruments within the orchestration and concentrate on their activity. Listen to the dynamics of the music and feel the tensions and releases. The voice-leadings are the references, the guides to understanding how the music is evolving.

Chord structures are assemblages of notes conceived and/or sounded simultaneously. The voice leadings within these assemblages continue to function as described.

Imagine a person in a room, let a second person enter the room and see that the mind seeks to create a relation between the two persons; note how the mood changes when a relationship is felt. When a third person appears there are further changes plus a dynamic, which was not before apparent. A good theatrical play contains these modulations of feeling and juxtaposing of ideas presented by the chosen characters and proposes them to the audience. A chord structure can be viewed as an assembly of persons with a multitude of possible relationships between them, active like characters in a play or film.

Think of each person as an assemblage of energy patterns which are intertwining themselves around a particular centre of three part thinking, feeling and willing; now see or hear each three note chord as a representation of that three part thinking, feeling and willing. It is well possible, by feeling the dynamics of music, to see those same dynamics in and between people.

HY: Could you explain a little about the relationships and how they might come about?

JZ: When a note is created, it is created by an instrument be it voice, guitar, violin etc. The quality of that instrument's sound is dictated by the construction of the instrument, where it is played and the manner in which it is attacked. When a guitar is sounded you hear the principal sound, the note that is held and played, and also secondary notes, somewhat quieter but which are created by the way that the different parts of the instrument resonate. These secondary notes are heard as overtones or partials and make up the tone of the note that we recognize as a guitar note.

An organic structure is in principle the same. An amoeba is organically simple and would produce simple sounds; a human being is a complex structure and produces very complex sounds.

With each human being there is a basic character trait supported by a multitude of secondary characteristics that an observer of that being can feel and even infer. If we put together two notes simultaneously on the guitar we hear the two notes but also we are aware of a blending of the overtones and partials of the two notes as some of these partials belong to both notes. If the two notes are played separately there is a recognizing, by the listener, of these resonating partials and an understanding of the relationship between them. It is exactly on a par with two people who meet; each has predominant characteristics and has from history and intent, overtones and partials which, when in the presence of similar overtones and partials in the other person, resonate and are enlivened. If the two people share more of the same frequency partials than fewer they will tend, by nature, to feel comfortable with each other. If they share fewer of the same frequency partials they will tend to feel uncomfortable.

When three people get together the new dynamics greatly increase the relational possibilities.

HY: The Holy Trinity again. I now understand why you would want to study voice leadings and chord structures and arrange them for guitar.

JZ: However, I had to start to earn which meant taking time to do that in which I had no real interest. In my mind I was prepared to do anything temporarily until a way into music appeared.

HY: Before we move on let us look at, as music notation and graph trajectories, a example taken from the charts that you were studying:

The letters A B C D E F G (white keys on a piano keyboard) refer to the root note on which each triad is built. Here the "C" triad is the reference with the other chords moving to and from it.

The black notes are the common links shared between pairs of triads. The red notes are the dynamic notes which move between each pair of triads. The 3 examples show how to move from any triad to any other. Each note of the music appears as a bar on the graph.

Example 1 The movement is smooth, calm

Example 1. Cycle 3. 1 note moves. 2 common notes

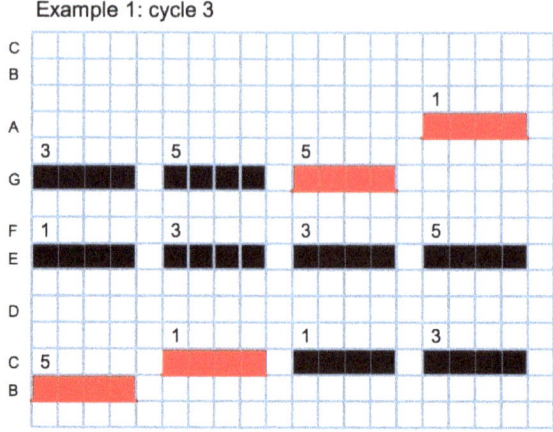

Example 2 The movement is animated but there is a common element

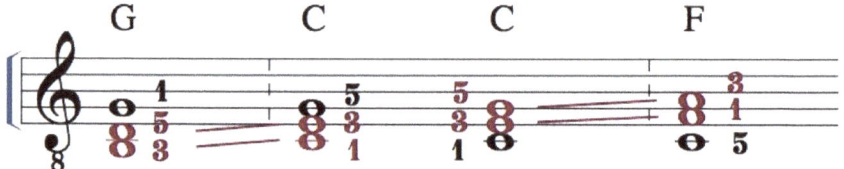

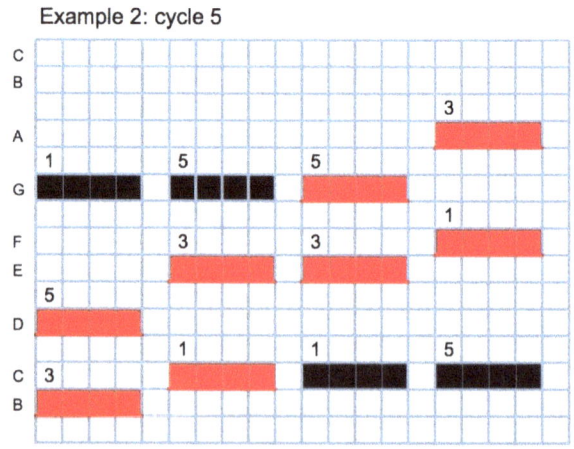

Example 3 The movement is is very dynamic with every element different

Example 3. Cycle 7. All 3 notes move. 0 common notes

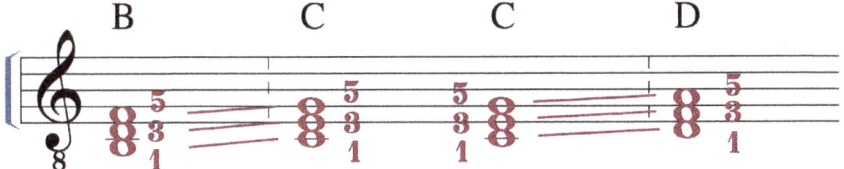

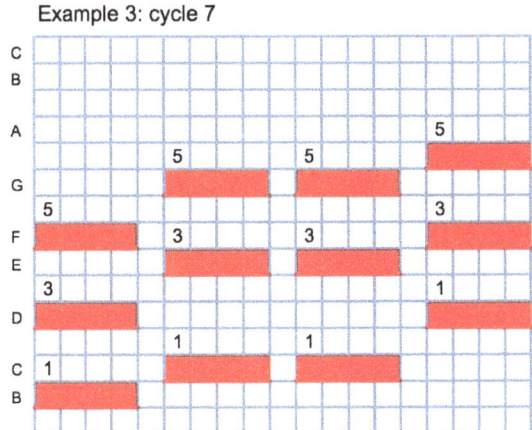

HY: You started to work for an insurance company?

JZ: Yes. It is ironic, the complete opposite of what I was looking for. My training there was to formulate policies so that a claim was impossible unless additional sums for 'special perils' were added to the premium to cover the many hazards and dangers that I was taught to look for or invent. Assuredly, for me, a "not to be missed" experience.

♃ ♄ ☿

Personal Journey

Chapter 10

Don Lord

"The profound meaning of music's essential aim… is to produce a communion, a union of man with his fellow man with the Supreme Being"

Igor Stravinsky (1882-1971)

Don Lord at Tan-y-Garth Hall

Don Lord, né Donald Sinclair Lord, born in 1926 in Burnley, was a lifelong friend and student of Eugene Halliday. He was aged sixteen when, as a student at the Manchester School of Art, he first met Eugene, aged thirty. Eugene had already left the Art School, but went to see an exhibition there and met Don. Drafted into the Army

in 1944, Don completed only two years at art school but, in the army, he received full officer training and was, by the end of the war, a warrant officer.

He and Eugene kept up a correspondence throughout the war, and when "demobbed", Don went to join Eugene and friends, in Manchester. These friends happened to be painters, musicians, dancers, actors etc. They were soon joined by specialists from the scientific and medical fields and were the nucleus of what was to become "Ishval".

Away from the art school Don developed other talents, especially with language and hermeneutics (study and interpretation of religious and philosophical texts). He studied assiduously texts of all major religions to understand for himself their different significances and also to resolve the contradictory interpretations offered by established churches.

Don, in a straightforward way unencumbered by academic detail, could get right to the nub of what is needed to communicate in most languages.

Between October 1992 & 2011 he was Director of Studies of the IHS. He was a leading Esperantist and from 1995 to 2000 he held the post of the John Buchanan Lecturer in Esperanto at Liverpool University. In 2006, the Esperanto Association of Britain published his "Conversational Esperanto - Lively Dialogues from Everyday Life", which is still in print. He died in 2012.

♃ ♄ ☿

HY: You were working in insurance when you met Don. How did you get together?

JZ: By reaching together. I was with John Resek, violinist, school friend and neighbour, browsing various bookshops for religious and philosophical literature. In one shop we were pointed to a section where I saw a copy of the Bhagavad-Gita. Without paying much attention to what was around me I reached for the book, not noticing that simultaneously another hand was doing the same thing. This resulted in the paperback edition being removed from the shelf by the two hands (weight of the book light but contents heavy!). Both owners of said hands looked at each other and burst out laughing. The other hand belonged to Don who asked what my interest was with the subject. After talking briefly Don suggested that I do some work on the book and, if I had any questions on the text, give him a call to discuss them. About a week later I had some questions, telephoned him and went with John Resek to Number 9 Wellington Road, Manchester. Don received us, and over supper, which he prepared, we discussed what we had been working on since our two-handed meeting. He proposed meeting up on a weekly basis, which we did, usually on a Friday or Saturday. He always prepared supper for us and we discussed, often until the early hours of the morning, what we had studied through the week—and more. Then one evening, having got to know each other better, Don just said to me: "Well, what is it you really want to do?" I replied that I wanted to be a musician, a guitar player, and he said, "Well, why don't you be it?"

The way he asked let me see absolutely what I wanted to do, allowed me to see that I could be a musician, it was like curtains opening on a stage and I just saw that I could say yes, I will be a musician, which I did.

The curtains closed, but it was too late to go back, I had already committed myself to a new life with the guitar, and understood at that moment, that I had been listening to negative advice for a long, long time and had almost forgotten that I could make my own free, positive decisions.

HY: The curtains opened and then they closed too fast for fearful egotism to make its appearance.

JZ: Don made clear that my choice was not an easy one and that a silk purse is not made out of a sow's ear overnight; but he did add that, if I agreed to his helping me on the way, he would do so, and he was forever as good as his word.

HY: Yes.

JZ: There were no musicians in my immediate family circle and my parents were frightened on my behalf because they had no personal experience of life in the arts.

They had sought advice for me from people, working in various fields but not from anyone actually involved in music. They could understand how a musician could earn with an orchestral instrument or piano but not with the guitar. The more they talked to people working in established occupations the more established occupations were suggested as good careers for me to take up and, in turn, the more frustrated and depressed I became.

Don had asked me simply what I wanted to do and when I told him, equally simply, he posed the question "Well, why not do that?" As he said that and I saw that I could do it, all the encumbering negativity disintegrated.

HY: He spoke to your true centre.

JZ: There was no doubt that my choice was correct because with the positive commitment I immediately felt better.

I also felt, and still do, that if a person really has something to accomplish there is an obligation to try to do it. There seems to be no point in passing some eighty years or so waiting for death, doing superficial, peripheral things without interest and which return no satisfaction; it is better just to pass away and free up some space for others.

The real point here is not that of the guitar, or any other particular activity, it is that each one of us needs to feel his own talents, whatever they are, and work to evolve them, to make them grow. Eugene repeated that each and every person has some talent and has a duty to develop it.

Search for, pursue your own life and follow that. Let it tell you what is right and wrong; for each one of us it is different. As Eugene often would say, make your way by letting it appear, do not interfere with it, let it grow before your eyes, step back and look at it, see where it is, review where it came from, how it got there, and be open to where it might be going. My key has been through the guitar, for another it might be piano or painting or even accountancy! Each one of us, on the inside, has a key to turn. I cannot recommend anything better to do.

♃ ♄ ☿

Don Lord (right) as remembered by John Zaradin at the time of his first meeting.

Don Lord (left) with friends Qinggen Xu & Tony Duckworth, not concerned by having their backs to the wall.

Don Lord (below) as remembered by Hephzibah (youngest in the group) in the garden at Wellington Road with Geoff and Abel Stanion.

Personal Journey

Don Lord
Portrait by Eugene Halliday 1948

Personal Journey

Chapter 11

Ishvalian Overtures

9 & 7 Wellington Road, Manchester in winter

Photograph by Tom Jolliffe (possibly taken without gloves).
Attic, top left, was the initial meeting place to discuss the Bhagavad-Gita.

Personal Journey

The Bhagavad Gita

"It is better to live your own destiny imperfectly than to live an imitation of somebody else's life with perfection."

"Curving back within myself I create again and again."

"For the senses wander, and when one lets the mind follow them, it carries wisdom away like a windblown ship on the waters."

The Bhagavad Gita

Not Wellington Road, Manchester in winter

Music can "minister to minds diseased, pluck from the memory a rooted sorrow, raze out the written troubles of the brain, and with its sweet oblivious antidote, cleanse the full bosom of all perilous stuff that weighs upon the heart".

William Shakespeare, Macbeth, Act 5, Scene 3

HY: Let us look at the time of your reaching out for the Bhagavad-Gita, when you met Don and he introduced you to Eugene.

You would have been eighteen or nineteen years old.

JZ: After several sessions with Don and then finally meeting Eugene, I felt that there was a possibility, by being with them, of finding what I was looking for. I did not know, but I felt well and more integrated simply by having met them and hearing what they said and seeing what they did. They seemed to have a detached understanding with balanced feeling which gave me confidence. They were not advising me, as were others, to conform to ways of life in which I had no interest.

I had opened myself up to them, as much as I could at the time, and was ready, therefore, to listen to what they had to say.

HY: You and John Resek had weekly meetings with Don at Wellington Road, and you were holding fast onto the idea of becoming a musician. You have said that Don was responsible for your meeting Eugene. What were you expecting before you actually met him?

JZ: Don referred to Eugene all the time, and one evening said that he would like him to have a look at us. We went to number 33 Wellington Road and were met by David Mahlowe, who then introduced us to Eugene in the reception room. I did not know what to expect, but on meeting him, he was, I suppose, exactly as I would have expected had I been knowing what to expect, but more so. He was so still and kind.

HY: Yes,

JZ: Don asked me afterwards, what age I thought Eugene was and when I told him, greatly overestimating, he burst out laughing.

HY: How did the meeting affect you?

JZ: It greatly encouraged me to persist and find a way to become a musician. Although I was beginning to understand music theoretically, I realised that there was a lot of work to do to become a guitar player. My tuition had been sporadic and hybrid and I was basically self-taught. Also, violinists and pianists played from extensive tried and tested repertoires, but the guitarist did not; his catalogue of published original music was relatively small, and he relied mainly on arrangements of music which had been written for other instruments.

Don asked me which direction I wanted to take with the guitar. Despite the fact that at the time I had a steel string guitar, not nylon, something inside pushed me to say that I wanted to play the classical Spanish guitar. I was surprised because there were so few classical guitar players at that time, Andrés Segovia being the best known, and there were hardly any career roads already laid.

♃ ♄ ☿

Logo signature created by Eugene Halliday

John Zaradin

Personal Journey

Four-stringed guitar of Eugene Halliday

J. Cole Violin of Eugene Halliday

Personal Journey

The Neapolitan mandolin of Eugene Halliday

Personal Journey

Chapter 12

Preparation for the Road

*Gold album award winner for his recording "Concierto de Aranjuez"
by Joaquin Rodrigo*

"My personal favourite... on an LP with John Zaradin and Guy Barbier conducting the Philomusica of London".

Joaquin Rodrigo

Personal Journey

"The highest goal of music is to connect one's soul to their Divine Nature, not entertainment".

Pythagoras (569- 475 BC)

"Harmony sinks deep into the recesses of the soul and takes its strongest hold there, bringing grace also to the body & mind as well. Music is a moral law. It gives a soul to the universe, wings to the mind, flight to the imagination, a charm to sadness, and life to everything. It is the essence of order."

Plato (429-347)

Piccadilly Theatre, London

Reception after the Première of 'Man of La Mancha' with the music director Denys Rawson & Wendy and Sandra Hambleton.

HY: What happened next?

JZ: Having made my decision, I told my parents I was going to resign from the job that I had and I asked them if I could stay at home for six months, without earning, so that I could practice and get a scholarship. After some agitated discussion, my mother appeased my father and they agreed. The next day I went to the office, declared that I was leaving to become a musician and resigned on the spot.

At home, I prepared my work schedule as Don had suggested.

HY: What was the schedule?

JZ: Again, compression decompression; involute e(x)volute. Set up session times with breaks: get up at 8am, breakfast; start to practise at 9am and work to the clock for an hour and a half; take a break, continue until lunchtime; and then start up again on the clock for the afternoon sessions. The basic idea was focused concentration and followed by relaxation; again, alternating compression and decompression.

HY: Training you to approach the work as a project to accomplish.

JZ: It was a practical, real work project, but there was no internal contradiction because I could see the improvement in playing. I was enjoying it, even though it was physically and mentally tiring. I even started to study the flute and began to become aware of the connection between breathing and phrasing in music, which every wind player is obliged to do. The guitar is like the piano in that the player can physically continue to play notes without consciously synchronizing phrases and breath. After working with the schedule for four months, I applied for and won a scholarship, thanks to the help of both Don and Eugene.

When the music college term started I found somewhere to live, close to Wellington Road, and moved in.

In the meantime, Eugene and his wife Peg, together with David and

Zero Mahlowe moved to Parklands, Bowdon, Cheshire and Don moved from Number 9 to 33. Not long afterwards, I also moved into 33 and lived there until I started to work in London in 1968.

HY: Your move to 33 Wellington Road would have been in 1964 or 1965 and was the house into which Don had moved.

♃ ♄ ☿

Personal Journey

Chapter 13
Making a Way Near and Far

Chemin de Guitardou

Could a guitar player resist such an address? (Way of the sweet guitar)

Chemin de Guitardou-s and don'ts.

Personal Journey

"In ancient times music was the foundation of all the sciences. Education was begun with music with the persuasion that nothing could be expected of a man who was ignorant of music."

Cicero (106-43 BC)

"Emotions of any kind can be evoked by melody and rhythm; therefore music has the power to form character."

Aristotle (384-322 BC)

John Zaradin and Noëlle enjoying a moment between concerts

Captain's party on a QEII transatlantic crossing.

HY: What was your work on the college course?

JZ: The classical guitar was still felt to be a novelty instrument, but the principal of the college saw that it could, like the piano, double in concert programmes both for solos and for accompanying a singer or other instrumentalist, thereby adding variety to the usual voice and piano format. This again was invaluable, positive experience.

At the suggestion of Don and Eugene I started to prepare music with John Resek; we put together a "music speciality" cabaret spot, as it was then defined, and started to work with different agents out of Manchester. Our circuit of dates expanded and included the "must play" *City Varieties Theatre* in Leeds.

A summer season of Sunday concerts at the *Ocean Room, Blackpool Tower*, gave us good press reviews, which we used to contact other agents.

Eventually we learned that many artists were going to West Germany on contracts to play for the American forces there. I had studied German at school and was more than ready to go and test it out.

There were two contracts on offer, one was for a weekly salary and play as required, the other was paid by individual show. The second option paid more on a pro rata system, but you never knew how much you were going to earn; we opted for the weekly sum and did not mind how many shows we would play, which in the end was quite a lot.

HY: Because you were working out of the UK, you missed your final examinations at music college.

JZ: Yes. The choice was either to stop working in order to get a diploma that would ostensibly open up opportunities for work, or continue working, as I already was.

I was determined to become a performing musician. I did not envisage supporting myself from teaching, for which diplomas were necessary.

There was a possibility, suggested by the college to take the examinations later in that year. I was again away working, and so I never completed the course.

A major change occurred at the beginning of 1968 when I was invited to play a concert at the Purcell Room, in London. Zero Mahlowe contacted her brother Philip Jones and his wife Ursula, who offered me a room at their house while I was in London for the concert.

HY: That is Philip Jones, trumpet player and founder of the *Philip Jones Brass Ensemble*, and his wife Ursula who managed the English Chamber Orchestra?

JZ: That is right. Then in Spring of 1968 *Man of La Mancha*, a musical play based on the novel *Don Quixote* by Miguel Cervantes, came to London from New York. The English Chamber Orchestra management had the contract to book the players for the show and Eugene strongly advised that I audition for the guitar part. This I did and was offered the stage part, there being two guitars in the show; guitar one went on stage to do things and then returned to play with the orchestra, guitar two stayed with the orchestra.

Although I was inexperienced and nervous I enjoyed it tremendously. It was a very valuable experience with stage business, solo guitar and also orchestral playing. Following a conductor was not in the usual training for classical guitar players, who thereby missed out on the required discipline, but my early sortie with the double bass and the playing experience at the college meant that I was not a complete novice. Each conductor brings to an orchestra his own interpretation of the music, and the orchestral musician must, unlike the soloist, abandon his own ideas for those of the conductor.

HY: What did the stage part require you to do?

JZ: Play the overture with the orchestra and then immediately go on stage to open the show with idiomatic sad flamenco and return to the orchestra. There were many on-stage scenes which included the guitar for both ambience playing and to accompany particular songs; there was one song to accompany where the guitar player was held in the air by dancer-actors while they followed the singer around the stage. It was stage business, not acting but a little bit unusual for a classical guitar player. The show ran for eight months of eight shows a week, was a success and I got used to working and living in the West End. The hybrid guitar part involved the whole gamut of techniques: classical, flamenco and orchestral plus the stage part. The experience was giving me the confidence I needed to feel that I could continue working there.

The time was very much the "Swinging 60s" and there was a lot of work on offer if one was in the right place.

After so many early years suffering dissuasion and negativity, I could hardly believe that I was surviving well by playing the guitar and that the life I had earlier imagined had become a reality. I really was enjoying the experience but, because it was all new, I was not as careful as I might have been and burned myself out somewhat. London is an entertainment centre with musicians, actors, dancers, agents, producers continuously meeting each other, searching for, trading and offering work possibilities. Television used music live at this time. The business was very competitive, but everyone I met seemed to be enjoying the challenges and looking for new experiences and relationships. People were not afraid to test things out.

To be getting home at 4 or 5 o'clock in the morning was fairly normal.

Whenever there was an opportunity to get to Manchester, I would telephone Eugene and ask if he could see me. He always seemed to be able to say yes, and each time, I would see him to explain what I had been doing. More often than not, he would pick up on what I had intended to discuss with him without my having to tell him first.

♃ ♄ ☿

Eugene Halliday early 1980s.

Late 1940s 9 Wellington Road.

Noëlle's home was in London a few hundred yards away from mine, but we did not meet until ten years later.

Noëlle, in the early '60s at the time when she was working, behind the scenes in London, on the design of the "Triffids" for the film "The Day of the Triffids".

Personal Journey

Chapter 14

Universal to Particular

Ovation Legend Classical Guitar

Synthetic back & sides for very stable tuning in variable temperatures.

Elemental Fire, Earth, Air & Water in the conception of the Ovation Guitar

In 1966, engineer and guitar virtuoso Charles Kaman, searching to find the sound "he always knew but never heard", created the **Ovation** guitar as an instrument that would clearly project an individual voice.

In realizing his guitar he worked with four fundamental elements: Sound, Shape, Substance and Soul, which could be read as Fire, Air, Earth and Water. He saw the instrument as a blank canvas or, for a metaphysician, an un-egoic sentient being in discovery of itself.

Here is a paraphrasing of the essence of Kaman's conception, which he has used to *describe his Ovation guitar. He sought:*

in Sound, consistent live balanced tones that articulate clearly and move the listener.

in Shape, form that reflects the function and unites the aural experience with the visual.

in Substance, control of the instrument by combining modern and traditional materials and expanding its tonal palette, dynamic range and durability.

in Soul, to open up the player's feeling so that his imagination is free to envisage and realise the music hidden within him.

♃ ♄ ☿

HY: The idea behind *Personal Journey* is not to write a biography of each person, but rather to look at particular ideas, feelings and events that have occurred in his or her life and which reflect the influence of Eugene Halliday.

So what did Eugene teach you and what did you learn from him?

JZ: I know that he taught me much more than I could consciously learn.

If one were to look at any series of events in my life and have some idea of what I have been trying to do, then to greater or lesser degrees the influence of Eugene, because of its universality, would be seen in all of it.

When there are crossroads in life and I am unsure of what to do, I look at my personal memories of Eugene and remember our sessions together. Next, I ask myself what he might have said in a given situation in order to simplify a problem and clarify the elements involved. After that I dip into his writings and read the text, keeping in mind the problem to be solved.

It is most strange that when a decision is then made based on what he might have done or said, that decision and the responsibility for it is felt completely as my own; it does not feel as though I have sought a solution from a third party. I freely accept the outcome of that decision. I have committed myself and have become free in that commitment.

HY: Given that a being wishes to understand himself and develop his unique talents and individuality, it follows that his road to fulfillment is going to be different from that of others. What did Eugene say to you about the gaining of experience?

JZ: He said that there is value in all experience. Eugene from time to time quoted Socrates: *"the unexamined life is not worth living"*, affirming that a true understanding of our lives is acquired by reflecting on our own experiences and our responses to them. Studying the life of another it is to be done always with an awareness of oneself making that study. By this, we can enrich our own lives with knowledge gained and significance gleaned from the activities of another person. At the same time, we are able to learn about ourselves by reflecting on what we might have done, or would do, given similar circumstances. Two for the price of one, how good does it get?

HY: Did you find that in marriage?

JZ: Yes. Early on with Eugene, I asked him about marriage and, with a smile, he answered *"women are all the same, so choose a good one"*.

Yet again an occasion when I knew what he meant without understanding what he had said!

Having spent more than enough years as a "strolling player" in search of the elusive woman, I gave up on the idea of trying to marry a domestic life with music. In order to earn as a guitar player I needed to travel, which I loved doing anyway. When not on tour, I was locked away at home learning new repertoire and preparing for the next tour or show. I began to feel that it was unfair to impose such a life on anyone and almost impossible to build a marriage. I say *almost impossible*, because I was pressed over several months by the singer Gillian Humphreys, with whom I was working, to meet Noëlle. When, thanks to Gillian's persistence, I eventually did, I knew that I had found, in Noëlle, someone who understood what it meant to work in the arts, spending limitless hours creating and crafting a piece of music; as a painter herself, she was doing the same with her own work. No explanation was needed if either of us worked through the night in order to get something "right". We were well together for some thirty three years, before she died in November 2013.

We had contradictory but complementary temperaments that seemed to work together and I was fortunate to find someone with whom to be freely bound in a timeless relationship.

Author Rudolph Fischer with Noëlle and John Zaradin aboard the QE2 exchanging writings for recordings.

There was a resonance with Noëlle similar to that which I had had with Eugene. Simply being in the presence of either opened mental and emotional doors and caused me to centre myself. They both encouraged a self-reflection which was enriching. When Eugene was in direct relation with someone he seemed always to accept and affirm the declared activity and intent of that person who would eventually come to see clearly what he or she was doing, and would then be free to decide to continue down the same road or change course.

If Eugene were to say to me, at one moment in time, that I ought to try everything once but save permanent injury and death to be the last things to try, I would understand this to be a personal comment to me at that time, not a universal directive. Another being may not need such a series of experiences.

If there is a general principle here it is, therefore, not to be afraid to try anything once, but re-affirm at each instance that what you are doing is what you, in your innermost centre, choose.

HY: I remember that he would often say not to prematurely destroy one's vehicle of experience. That said, he used to talk about testing things to destruction.

JZ: As advice for me, that might have been too dangerous. I was already in danger of self-destruct without advice.

HY: Did he give you advice?

JZ: Only if I were ready to advise myself. Generally he would simply ask a question in such a way that I learned what I needed to be doing in answering his question. Whenever he asked something I would always be aware of many possible answers plus that which was the correct one.

HY: Let each will see where it is going and if it looks off course re-direct it back onto itself. Simple efficiency.

JZ: Yes, realistic and a 100% positive. A free will can feel the state of other wills and will offer possibilities of release for those wills if that is what they are looking for. It cannot do more.

♃ ♄ ☿

Personal Journey

From the Gallery of Noëlle Brassac Zaradin

Personal Journey

Personal Journey

Chapter 15

Coda

A Nocturne at Chemin de Guitardou

"Man's music is seen as a means of restoring the soul, as well as confused and discordant bodily afflictions, to the harmonic proportions that it shares with the world soul of the cosmos."

Plato (Timaeus) (429-347 BC)

Personal Journey

It is said that, in order to experience being truly centred in that free-dome, any attachment to personal thinking, feeling or willing must consciously be withdrawn, including even those treasured ideas acquired from any person or external source which, in varying circumstances, act as references for security. Any action from a memory of what has been said or done is a danger to freedom. Jesus Christ himself said that one is obliged to give up everything.

A useful technique in achieving this freedom is to turn your attention from any stimulus and, gathering yourself together, look-feel-hear for your soul-self searching for nothing, which is that real internal un-stimulated space where you will find an authoritative nothing, and be more than happy to do so.

In everyday speaking we seem to understand each other by paying attention to concatenations of consonants and can often forget that there are spaces in between those consonant characters. Ideas can also take our attention and cause us to forget that they owe their existence to our awareness of the space around them. Look for and feel this space and see the forms within it.

The Musician, as Artist, is continually aware that his music is willed into substantially compressed notes from this decompressed space.

The case is closed.

♃ ♄ ☿

HY: You were realizing the idea that you had to travel the world. You felt emotionally stable doing it and had practical skills with music and the guitar.

Were you continually aware of your education with Eugene and Don as your life evolved or did you put it to one side when you seemed to be getting your own way and then return to it when things were difficult?

JZ: Yes to both questions. There are intentions and drives within us, which are mere distractions and dissolve of their own accord when seen to be such. There are also deeper, difficult-to-see memories that are held onto unconsciously and which are real determinants; these produce smoke screens if we try to examine them, but are chains if freedom is our aim. They seem to be part of our make up, and we feel that we would lose our proper identity if we freed ourselves from them. Because of this they are much harder to deal with. They are real obstructions to a free life and need to be seen and understood as the restrictions that they are. However, we said earlier that although life does not give us what we think we want, it always produces what we need for our development. If we genuinely prefer to understand and be free from our habitual conditioned selves, it will happen. Life will create, for each one of us, situations that offer the possibility of rethinking, reviewing and re-centring ourselves. It will confront us repeatedly with the consequences of a wrong decision, that is a decision that ties us into enslaving and repetitive behavior, until the problem is seen and the right choice, that is a choice which liberates us, is made. There is no morality here: if we wish freedom then we must make choices which give us that; if we wish slavery we make choices which lead to that. There is an inevitable logic to the fact that life will confront us repeatedly with the consequences of a wrong decision; it is that a wrong decision is an enclosing action, it locks the energy into going round and round until the binding becomes so dense that we risk never escaping. If we become so bound, the possibility of becoming a consciously self-aware essential being is greatly reduced. William Blake said, *"Kiss the joy as it flies"*, one meaning of which is to see the formal display but do not attach to it. A wrong decision is only wrong in its capturing of energy and inducing identification. If our preference is for freedom, then although the locking of energy in itself is not wrong, it can be said to be so if it causes identification and reduced liberty.

HY: How does the process of growing out of the ego-self into a consciously self-aware essential being happen?

JZ: It must be by the choices made by each individual. For myself, it begins by examining my choices, withdrawing energy from those existing choices that I see to be enslaving or of no value and then by feeling very carefully into a new awareness of myself, a new level of being.

With a commitment to do so, each individual can play out his history in time and decide to detach himself or herself, or not, from any restrictive determinants.

At each new level of awareness I see internally something die and then something new start to evolve.

As life progresses, we can realise that, apart from our own essential thinking, feeling and willing, we are composed of inherited purposes and also of wants and desires created by environment, education and social life.

With each new developmental step that we take, with every essential choice that we make, we are released from some inertias of our past and start to become familiar with ourselves in our new state. No matter how sincere we are in our choices, there is energy operating for the benefit of the ego until one is 100% not afraid of 'no-thing'. If one is not at least equally aware of both something and nothing the scales will tip for something.

Until a problem is grown into and felt and understood, it cannot be grown out of. There is no easy trick to learn and actually realise no-thing in something. Good education is a preparation for this realization, but it will not in itself produce it. Each individual, being differently composed, must see and internally realize the logic of his or her real position. How an individual centres himself is his or her own choice. My authority for developing my composition, that is my own life, and its differently functioning parts is mine and mine alone, as is the choice to modify those parts for a better functioning, or even to put the composition on one side when its developmental possibilities seem to be logically exhausted. To maintain well-being, I must also accept responsibility for all decisions made.

I can only be suspicious of those powers evident in the world, which increasingly undertake to mind everyone's business. They are seen to organize themselves to impose conformity in the name of social stability and to manipulate external education to fix people in functions suitable to those powers.

"Tis so,' said the Duchess: 'and the moral of that is — "Oh, 'tis love, 'tis love, that makes the world go round!"'

'Somebody said,' Alice whispered, 'that it's done by everybody minding their own business!'

'Ah, well! It means much the same thing,' said the Duchess.

Alice's Adventures in Wonderland, Chapter 9

It can be observed that those who like to define laws for others tend to be themselves fearful and imagine chaos if they cannot restrict others with externally imposed definitions and repetitious practices. Whenever such persons are asked if they, unrestricted, would behave chaotically, the answer is always no, not me, but the others. It is always the others who cannot control themselves. Personal fears and fantasies are assumed onto others because fearful people attach themselves for security, onto external systems and structures instead of their own internal centres.

Even though it can be seen that there are those who will to divisive and separative appropriation, my own experiences guide me to feel that, in general, people prefer to work together for mutual benefit, and enjoy that sense of well-being that arises within from doing so.

Eugene always said that all must be accepted and *all* includes the dreadful as well as the joyful. All is all to 100%. There are those who, for their own purposes, refer to *all* as *all* within a concept defined or left undefined. As an example: in France, where we are, we see on a shop door, "ouvert tous les jours sauf dimanche" (open every day except Sunday). This shows that every day, does not mean every day, but every day that someone has himself decided that he will work, which in this case excludes Sunday. Here, all means all the elements within the concept, not *all all*. For us, Ishval et al, for the student of reality and beyond, *all* is *all* and that includes even no-thing.

The ideas and work of Eugene Halliday are ideas and work which enable a psyche or soul, to create for itself a free-dome reference centre of its own thinking, feeling and willing, from which it can view reality unconditioned by external stimuli or its own internal particular inheritance of inertias. Eugene Halliday explains clearly, in all of his writings, how to become free, and he is unique in his way of preparing the mind to become aware of no-thing as something which is or can become real. He clarifies, to anyone who can read or listen to what he wrote or said, how to be free to evolve one's own talents. His work illustrates how to be free of mechanical behavior. His *"reflexive self-consciousness"*, his *"the observer is not the observed"*, are such simple ideas which can be applied and understood by anyone wishing to apply and understand them. The genius is in the simplicity; it is almost impossible not to understand what he says given the will to understand him.

Whenever I was with Eugene I found myself continually, automatically and willingly cross-checking my motives. His presence and tone of voice caused me to ask myself what I was doing and why; I found myself making judgements about my own thinking, feeling and willing and finally realised that I was not that perfect being that I imagined the world saw me to be. I decided to accept that, and, instead of trying to piece together a broken image of a life in reality assembled by ignorance, and reactive naïve behaviour, I started to look inside to uncover whatever talents I might have and to work on them to the best of my ability. This decision released me from the past and gave me that sense of freedom and well-being with the world that I now cherish.

When a person becomes so tired of the internal slavery to memory, the living death of inertia, the clinging to self-conceiving, then that person is already growing out of those things and has begun to slough off the habit of dependency on fearful memories and irrational inhibitors. There appears an awareness of simply being which is that non-dual field of no-thing that Eugene Halliday, like no one else, explains with breathtaking logic, clarity and sensitivity.

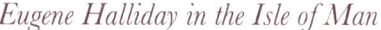

Eugene Halliday in the Isle of Man

Personal Journey

Eugene Halliday circa 1950s by Peter Gunning via Ruth Templeton

Eugene Halliday by Leslie Lord brother of Don Lord

Personal Journey

The theme 'Easter Song' composed by Eugene Halliday is here arranged as a duet for lead line and guitar

Easter Song

Eugene Halliday arranged by John Zaradin

Eugene Halliday: Biographical Notes

Eugene Halliday was an accomplished artist, writer and speaker who came to be recognised as a teacher of philosophy and a proponent of not only the idea but also the fact that each and every individual is essentially responsible for that life in which they are centred and owe it to themself to develop that life. His teaching was to show that self-conscious reflexion and integrated focusing of one's energies will allow the individual to become aware of an internal life force which is its own real and natural authority.

Born in 1911, Eugene's parents were Music Hall artistes: his father a violinist, his mother a singer. They gave him an unusual education which, doubtlessly, would have aided his ability to understand, relate and interpret concepts of philosophy, psychology, scriptures of major religions and the science of his day.

He studied at the Manchester School of Art from 1928 and in the 1930s worked for Allied Newspapers as an illustrator and cartoonist. During WW2 he was a conscientious objector and worked as a commercial artist. His work was shown in the Manchester Academy of Fine Art and other galleries, and he began giving talks on philosophy. Soon he became the catalyst for a community of creative people, which included refugees from Nazi Germany. This led to the founding of two organisations, the International Hermeneutic Society (I.H.S.) and the Institute for the Study of Hierological Values (Ishval).

In the mid-1960s Eugene moved to Cheshire. He continued to write, lecture and devise classes for self-developmental work, with the aim of refining sensitivity and heightening consciousness, until his death in 1987. He was a man wholly dedicated to the development of the potential of his fellow beings—which was his definition of Love.

♃ ♄ ☿

Personal Journey

Chapter 16

Personal Reflections on a Personal Journey

John Zaradin

Evening view from the terrace at Chemin de Guitardou

Personal Journey

These following notes are not part of conversations with Hephzibah, but are part of my Personal Journey made possible by the hand of Eugene Halliday.

♃ ♄ ☿

Time to go within, sense the field compressions and decompressions and listen

"The encounter with nothingness, an experience of the intellect in its pursuit of Truth, is an encounter with that which necessarily transcends intellect and yet is the Ultimate of all experiences. But Nothingness is but No-thing-ness, the essence of what it means to be 'not a thing'. A 'thing' is a consolidated precipitate or modality of Infinite Sentient Power. It is thus a negation. Yet it is a reference centre for this sentient power, and a standpoint from which a view of reality may be gained finitely as opposed to the infinite view of the infinite sentient power as it is to itself in its infinity."

Eugene Halliday, Contributions From a Potential Corpse, Book IV, page 102

Reflection: If I reflect my present state of being into any past time, then future probable and possible courses of action can be seen. If I consciously reflect on a memory, I can look at how I was feeling at the time of the event which created the memory and see feelings and ideas of which I was unaware when the event occurred.

Sincere self-reflection clarifies innermost motives and allows them to be re-determined.

♃ ♄ ☿

Motive: If I can see my true motives as they really are, restrictive egotistical conditioning falls away and dies.

Much of Eugene's work was in explaining to others how to become reflexively self-conscious and free of such binding conditioning.

♃ ♄ ☿

Choice: Each time a determining decision is consciously made, there is a re-aligning and balancing of internal energies which give rise to a re-conceiving of the self. If I make a correct decision there is a sense of liberation and positivity, but if I make an incorrect decision I feel ill at ease and negative. A correct decision offers a solution to a problem which then ceases to be a determining factor, but an incorrect decision compounds the problem.

At a certain point, I realised that I change myself by my choices and become much more careful with my choosing.

♃ ♄ ☿

Character: New experience changes the dynamics of the character and necessitates a re-balancing as the changes are absorbed. In a positive case, the newly aware self can feel at a loss, disorientated, because its references are different. The more conscious I become of these natural changes the more I feel at ease with them and discover a stability in the expectancy of not knowing. If I continue to *know*, I suspect my inner motives and re-examine them.

Character is formed by the will continuously and repeatedly creating and re-creating behavior patterns. The character can become charred in time and burn itself out as its formal usefulness is outgrown. When this happens, I can then, consciously detach from identification with those habits (behaviour patterns) and look to find myself anew. The essential will-awareness of the character detaches itself when the value to it of its form is exhausted. When it detaches, it does so naturally into the realization of a subtler level of awareness where, because of the habit of identifying with a grosser form, it can feel lost, aimless, without purpose, unable to find itself in the new more subtle form. The temptation here is to return, out of fear, to the security of old habits and to try to re-instate what has been put on one side. At this moment I must decide to trust in my will to find myself and ignore any fear that arises. Because there are no recognizable references in the new state, the only security is in no-thing and in the logic that if there is no-thing there is nothing harmful in that no-thing because there is nothing there that can be harmful.

♃ ♄ ☿

Faith: Eugene spoke of faith as that by which a person can, by focused thinking, feeling and willing, gather together his or her energies to achieve a goal. He advocated one hundred percent faithful concentration in order to push the will until the goal is achieved and the true logic of the will's position is exposed. He added that, at this point, the person becomes different by the experience but may not immediately recognize the fact. In order to overcome the disorientation caused by a new level of perception, it is recommended to be still until there is that balanced free feeling, which has resulted from faith applied as a power to work and achieve.

♃ ♄ ☿

Freedom: In freedom it is easy to accept another's point of view and work with it. In freedom there is a shared joy such as is experienced by musicians either between themselves or by a performer and audience.

♃ ♄ ☿

Significance and Form: When I respect a person, and would like to appropriate some of his qualities, I do not merely copy and mimic those qualities, but rather work at absorbing them and making them my own.

If a person repeats verbatim or copies the words of another (Eugene) without feeling the significance of that other's words, that is without correctly appropriating and understanding the logic of the ideas, then those words will only sound an opinion, distorting significance rather than reflecting it. The logic of the elements will be apparent but the speaker will not be at one with the relationships and significance of those elements.

However, it is always valuable and beneficial to feel into the lives of respected, integrated characters and personalities and try to understand and absorb the qualities that create that integration. By doing this one is raised in the direction of, and to the level of those qualities.

If those good ideas are shared, there is an opportunity for others to benefit from them.

Those who knew Eugene personally are able to imagine themselves in his position as "universal man" and wonder what he might have done, said or be feeling in any given situation. If I do this, I tend to become more aware of the significance of that situation rather than of its formal details.

Do not be distracted into trying to characterize or particularize Eugene or any other person but concentrate rather on asking yourself why you have such an interest in those characterizations and particularizations.

♃ ♄ ☿

Relating: A non-conditioned free relationship is a natural process often experienced between artists and is the reason that, for example, musicians so readily give themselves to the interplay of sounds and dynamics when they perform. The more freely aware the composer/

performer, the more the listener is lifted to appreciate qualities in himself that he would not usually feel without listening to that interchange.

The music of Bach is an example of music which readily engages and elevates both performer and listener; the works of Shakespeare entertain the literary mind in a similar way.

♃ ♄ ☿

Music: Eugene said not to let the popular songs be dismissed without reflecting that, "they are expressions of many generations of trial & tribulation."

He also suggested that a performer who wishes to introduce new music in a concert, establish first a relationship with the audience by playing something familiar. When the listener is "tuned in" and at ease he will be prepared to open himself up to absorb a new piece or idiom.

When Eugene spoke, it was like a good instrumentalist playing a well known, tried and tested piece of music. His phrasing, timing and intent revealed new sensations and ideas which each listener received uniquely.

A good musician, in performance, reveals his own Self-centred awareness and opens up, in each listener, the possibility to be likewise centrally aware.

♃ ♄ ☿

A polished mirror: is a useful image to hold in relationship with Eugene Halliday as his written work serves as such a polished mirror if the reader will. A perfect crystal image is said to reflect truth because there is no distortion of the image reflected in it and, if we choose to reflect ourselves in this way, we might just see ourselves as we really are.

♃ ♄ ☿

Personal Journey

Adam (male half) by Eugene Halliday

Adam (female half) by Eugene Halliday

Personal Journey

Noëlle Brassac Zaradin

Personal Journey

GLOSSARY

Bach, Johann Sebastian

1685 – 1750. German composer.

Bax, Sir Arnold Edward Trevor KCVO

1883 – 1953. English composer and poet. His musical style blended elements of romanticism and impressionism, often with influences from Irish literature and landscape.

Bhagavad-Gita

A scripture which is part of the Hindu epic, the 'Mahabharata'. It is in the form of a dialogue between prince Arjuna and his charioteer, an avatar of the god Krishna. The Bhagavad Gita is among a number of sacred texts which Eugene Halliday recommended for study, along with the Tao De Ching, the works of William Blake, Jacob Boehme and the Bible.

Blake, William

1757–1827. English painter, poet and printmaker. He is now considered a seminal figure in the history of the poetry and visual arts of the Romantic Age. His prophetic poetry has been said to form "what is in proportion to its merits the least read body of poetry in the English language". His visual artistry led one contemporary art critic to proclaim him "far and away the greatest artist Britain has ever produced". He produced a diverse and symbolically rich oeuvre, which embraced the imagination as "the body of God" or "human existence itself".

Blavatsky, Helena Petrovna

1831 – 1891, born in Yekaterinoslav Russia, formerly as Helena von Hahn, was a Russian philosopher, and occultist. In 1875, Blavatsky, Henry Steel Olcott, and William Quan Judge established a research and publishing institute called the Theosophical Society. Blavatsky defined Theosophy as *"the archaic Wisdom-Religion, the esoteric doctrine once known in every ancient country having claims to civilization"*. One of the main purposes of the Theosophical Society was "to form a nucleus of the Universal Brotherhood of Humanity, without distinction of race, creed, sex, caste or color". Blavatsky saw herself as a missionary of this ancient knowledge.

Cambon d'Albi

A village three kilometres south of Albi, Tarn, France. Albi, eighty five kilometres north-east of Toulouse and was the site of the Albigensian Crusade in 1208 which slaughtered the population of the city in order to destroy the Cathar community, defined as heretics. The largest red brick cathedral in the world holds centre stage in Albi reminding visitors of the power that the Catholic church exercised in Europe at that time.

Cathars

Religious group which appeared in Europe in the eleventh century, said to originate in Persia or the Byzantine Empire, arriving in the South of France by way of the Balkans and Northern Italy. Records from the Roman Catholic Church mention them under various names and in various places. Catholic theologians debated with themselves for centuries whether Cathars were Christian heretics or whether they were not Christians at all. Roman Catholics still refer to Cathar belief as 'the Great Heresy' though the official Catholic position is that Catharism is not Christian at all. As Dualists, Cathars believed in two principles, a good creator god and his evil adversary (much like God and Satan of mainstream Christianity). Cathars called themselves simply Christians; their neighbours distinguished them as "Good Christians".

Cervantes, Miguel

Spanish author El Hombre de La Mancha, See 'Don Quixote'.

Chord cycle chart

Shows notes in a section of music functioning as a musical grammar.

Clegg, Maurice

Liverpool businessman, attended Eugene Halliday's lectures at Ishval. Author of an autobiography 'A Life' (2005), which has been described as a book which would help business people make a success of their lives.

Conover, Willis Clark, Jr.

1920 – 1996, was a jazz producer and broadcaster on the 'Voice of America' for over forty years. He produced jazz concerts at the White House, the Newport Jazz Festival, and for movies and television. By arranging concerts where people of all races were welcome, he is credited with helping to de-segregate Washington D.C. nightclubs. He is credited with keeping interest in jazz alive in the countries of Eastern Europe through his nightly broadcasts during the Cold War.

Coppola, Carmine

1910 – 1991. American composer, flautist, editor, musical director, and songwriter who contributed original music to The Godfather, The Godfather Part II, Apocalypse Now, and The Godfather Part III, all directed by his son Francis Ford Coppola.

Crowley, Aleister

1875 – 1947. English occultist, ceremonial magician, poet, painter, novelist, and mountaineer.

Don Quixote

Fully titled 'The Ingenious Gentleman Don Quixote of La Mancha' is a Spanish novel by Miguel de Cervantes Saavedra.

Published in two volumes, in 1605 and 1615, Don Quixote is considered the most influential work of literature from the Spanish Golden Age. It is said to have been translated into more languages than any book other than the Bible. It was the inspiration for the musical 'The Man of La Mancha' in which, for the London production, John Zaradin played the guitar part.

Dot (See also ' Line Simple')

Eugene Halliday continually worked to clarify his ideas and was particular to define the terms he used. In his presentations, 'nothing' (or rather 'no-thing' as contrasted with 'some-thing'), is represented by a blank sheet of paper. In this mode of thinking, the simplest appearance of 'any-thing' can be represented by a dot. The reference is to the most infinitesimal event that can appear within or out of 'no-thing'.

English Chamber Orchestra (ECO)

British chamber orchestra based in London. The full orchestra regularly plays concerts at Cadogan Hall, and the ECO Ensemble performs at Wigmore Hall. The orchestra regularly tours in the UK and internationally, and holds the distinction of not only having the most extensive discography of any chamber orchestra, but also of being the most well-travelled orchestra in the world; no other orchestra has played concerts in as many different countries as the ECO. Co-founded by Dr Ursula Jones, wife of the trumpeter Philip Jones, in 1960.

Engram

Means by which memory traces are stored as biophysical or biochemical changes in the brain (and other neural tissue) in response to external stimuli.

They are also sometimes conceived as a neural network or fragment of memory. Experiments are now showing that memory recordings appear not to be localized in the brain. The existence of engrams is posited by some scientific theories to explain the persistence of memory and how it is stored. The existence of neurologically defined engrams is not significantly disputed and research about them continues.

Fischer, Rudolph

Retired from his career in banking because the management took offence that he made jokes and laughed with banking clients. He had over the years made notes and produced *Klausche* as a book filled with anecdotes and perceptions and written in a *grand mélange* or better *tolle*

Mischung of German and English.

Freeman, Fred

1921-2007. In WW2 Major Fred Freeman served with the Chindits in Burma, under Orde Wingate. After the war he rejoined his family business, Freemans (Liverpool) Ltd, becoming Chairman in 1958. From 1974 he devoted a considerable amount of time to voluntary and charity work. His book 'The SUVOC Application' was influential in the adoption of payroll charity giving. As Chair and Honorary Director of United Voluntary Organisation, he was instrumental in its becoming affiliated with United Way of America in 1975. In 2007 he received an Honorary Degree of Doctor of Laws from the University of Liverpool, in recognition of his philanthropic work. A fund to relieve individual cases of poverty and hardship in Liverpool, was renamed 'The Fred Freeman People for People Fund' in his honour after his death. An annual lecture in his name was set up at Liverpool University, the first being given by Cherie Blair in 2010. Fred and his wife Yvonne met Eugene Halliday in the early 1960s, and with him founded the charity Ishval. Eugene and Fred co-authored the book 'Top Economy: Or Whole-group Good'. The Mr & Mrs F C Freeman Charitable Trust continued to support the work of Eugene Halliday throughout his lifetime, to support the charity Ishval until its closure in 2015, and to donate seed-funding to its successor organisation, the Eugene Halliday Association.

Gershwin, George

1898 – 1937, American composer and pianist.

Halliday, Eugene

1911-1987. Artist and writer. Founder of I.H.S. (q.v.) and ISHVAL (q.v.). Author of "Defence of the Devil", "Reflexive Self-Consciousness", "The Tacit Conspiracy" and other titles. Halliday's written and audio works are available for free download on eugenehallidayarchive.info, and transcripts of his audio lectures are available on eugene-halliday.net. For biographical material see eugenehalliday.net and for the Eugene Halliday Association see ehassociation.org.

Eugene Halliday Association

Eugene Halliday Association, founded 2014, a not-for-profit organisation created to continue the work of ISHVAL (q.v.), also known as the Eugene Halliday Society. The purpose of this was to simplify operations by ceasing to be a charity, and by revising its aims and objectives to make it clear that the work of the Association was centred on and guided by the work of Eugene Halliday.

Eugene Halliday Institute for the Study of Hierological Values

Renaming in 2009, of the Institute for the Study of Hierological Values, also known as ISHVAL (q.v.). Superseded by the Eugene Halliday Association (q.v.).

Eugene Halliday Society

A working name for the Eugene Halliday Institute for the Study of Hierological Values, also known as ISHVAL (q.v.). Superseded by the Eugene Halliday Association (q.v.).

I.H.S.

International Hermeneutic Society, founded in Liverpool in the 1950s by Eugene Halliday and Ken (later Khen) Ratcliffe. Hermeneutics is the art, theory or science of the interpretation of sacred texts (see also ISHVAL). The I.H.S. is now a charity based in North Wales. After Khen's death, Donald Lord became their Director of Studies until shortly before his death in 2012. The I.H.S. offers lectures, study groups and weekend courses. hermeneutic.co.uk

ISHVAL

Ishval, the Institute for the Study of Hierological Values. 'Hierology' means 'sacred literature' such as biblical and other religious texts. 'Hermeneutics' is the study—the art, theory or science of interpretation—of such texts (see also I.H.S.). Founded as an educational charity in 1964 by Eugene Halliday, Fred and Yvonne Freeman, David and Zero Mahlowe, its constitution was adopted on 31st August 1966. Funded by the Mr & Mrs Freeman Charitable Trust, a band of loyal Covenanters, and continuing donations, Ishval operated in 'Parklands', a house in Bowdon, Cheshire, until 1994, offering monthly lectures, readings, plays and a variety of classes. The house provided, in addition, a home for Mr and Mrs Halliday and Mr and Mrs Mahlowe; a base for Mr Halliday's psychotherapeutic practice; and the home of the Melchisedec Press, founded by David Mahlowe, through which he published the works of Eugene Halliday, in particular the hardback Collected Works. Since 1994 meetings, classes and lectures have been held in a variety of venues. The charity was renamed the Eugene Halliday Institute for the Study of Hierological Values in 2009 and was known latterly as the Eugene Halliday Society. Ishval ceased to be a charity in April 2015 in order to simplify operations and reformulate its aims and objectives. Its work continues as the Eugene Halliday Association (q.v.), a not-for-profit organisation.

Halliday, Margaret

Wife of Eugene Halliday, known as Peg.

Hardy, Bob

Musician, founder and administrator of the Eugene Halliday Archive eugenehallidayarchive.info

Hittite

Anatolian people, Indo-European 3000 BC

Humphreys, Gillian

See web site for full details of Gillian Humphreys. concordiafoundation.com/welcome/gillian-humphreys-biography.

Jeorrett, John

Engineer, printer and craftsman, was a friend of Eugene Halliday.

Jones, Philip and Ursula

The trumpeter Philip Jones OBE (1928-2000) was the brother of Zero Mahlowe. He and his wife Ursula Strebi Jones OBE were friends of Eugene Halliday. Philip was principal trumpet for six London Orchestras, and founded the Philip Jones Brass Ensemble in 1951. It was one of the first modern classical brass ensembles to be formed. The group played either as a quintet or, as a ten-piece for larger halls. It toured and recorded extensively, and numerous arrangements were commissioned, many of which were bequeathed on Jones' death to the library of the Royal Northern College of Music. Following Philip's retirement from his post as Principal of Trinity College of Music, a number of the members of his group continued, changing their name to London Brass. Ursula was co-founder of the English Chamber Orchestra (qv) and General Manager from 1960-1974, and Manager of the Philip Jones Brass Ensemble from 1974-1986. She holds a PhD in New World Archaeology, lectures on the pre-history of Mexico and is a Board Member of the Lucerne Festival and of Streetwise Opera.

Kaman, Charles Huron

1919 – 2011. Was an American aeronautical engineer, businessman, inventor and philanthropist, known for his work in rotary-wing flight and also in musical instrument design via the Kaman Music Corporation.

Kay, Albert

One of the first certified music teachers, in the UK, of the

'Joseph Schillinger System of Musical Composition'.

Lecuona y Casado, Ernesto

1895 – 1963. Cuban composer and concert pianist of worldwide fame. His compositions consist of zarzuela, Afro-Cuban Cuban rhythms and suites. Many songs became popular 'hits' and remain to this day as evergreens. Titles include: *Siboney (Canto Siboney)*, *Malagueña*, *The Breeze And I (Andalucía)* and *Always in my heart (Siempre en mi Corazón)*

Leeds City Varieties

Grade II* listed music hall in Leeds, West Yorkshire, England.

It was built in 1865 as an adjunct to the White Swan Inn (dating from 1748) in Swan Street and the original interior is largely unaltered. It is a rare surviving example of the Victorian era music halls of the 1850s/1860s. The interior is a long rectangle, with boxes separated by cast-iron columns along the sides at circle level. It became the 'City Palace of Varieties' with Charlie Chaplin, Marie Lloyd and Houdini being among the artists who performed there.

Between 1953 and 1983, the theatre achieved national fame as the venue for the BBC television programme 'The Good Old Days'.

Line, Simple (See also 'Dot')

Eugene Halliday continually worked to clarify his ideas and was particular to define the terms he used. In his presentations, 'no-thing' is represented by a blank sheet of paper; with this mode of thinking, the simplest appearance of 'any-thing' can be represented by a dot. The reference is to this point, the most infinitesimal event that can appear within or out of 'no-thing'. The next development that can happen is that a second dot appears, and then afterwards a third, fourth and so on. There is a real change when the series of dots appears in our mind as a line, an automatic sensing of space from the first dot to the last. We have also a sense of time when the mind switches its attention from one dot to another. A dramatic change occurs when the imagined series of dots wanders and turns across a space that it has previously traversed as the imagined line. This looping of itself creates an image and sense of an enclosure. This, in turn, gives rise to a sense of limited space, within the loop, and also to a sense of unlimited space, without or outside of the loop.

Lord, Don

1926 - 2012. See text Chapter Ten.

Mahlowe, David

1928 - 1998. Actor, Manchester Library Theatre, film, TV and radio. TV presenter and interviewer. ITV 'Tempo', ABC in the North, Ulster TV, 'What the Papers Say'. Founder Trustee of Ishval, literary executor and publisher of Eugene Halliday as Melchisedec Press.

Mahlowe, Zero

1930-2015. Wife of David Mahlowe. Actor (as Marah Stohl) Manchester Library Theatre, TV and radio. Founder Trustee of Ishval.

Mairants, Ivor

1908 - 1998. Jazz and classical guitarist, teacher and composer.

With his wife Lily in 1958 he created Ivor 'Mairants Musicentre', a specialist guitar store in London that was the first of its kind in the country and is still among the foremost of its kind in the UK.

Man of La Mancha

Successful Musical play of the 1960s. See 'Don Quixote'.

MIDI:

Musical Instrument Digital Interface.

In 1988 Alby James, director of the Temba Theatre Company, invited John Zaradin to compose and perform original music for his production of 'Romeo & Juliet', the setting of the play being transposed to Havana from Verona. The score was created for solo classical guitar controlling synthesizers, via MIDI (Musical Instrument Digital Interface), allowing orchestral colours and sound effects to be incorporated into the production. The music was performed live without any sequencing or pre-recording and demonstrated how computer technology could greatly expand the possibilities of the acoustic instrument. 'Caribbean Fantasy for Guitar' is the music from this production, compiled and arranged as a suite for solo guitar.

Miller, Glenn

1904 – *missing in action*, after leaving Bedford on December 15, 1944. American big band musician, arranger, composer, and bandleader.

Mozart, Wolfgang Amadeus

1756 – 1791. prolific and influential composer of the Classical era.

Mozart showed prodigious ability from his earliest childhood. Already competent on keyboard and violin, he composed from the age of five and performed before European royalty. At 17, he was engaged as a court musician in Salzburg. He was dismissed from this position in 1781 while on a visit to Vienna and decided to work from that capital. During his final years there he composed many of his best-known symphonies, concertos, operas and portions of the Requiem, which was largely unfinished at the time of his death. The circumstances of his early death are still in question. He was survived by his wife Constanze and two sons.

Ocean Room

Concert and recital room in the tower at Blackpool holiday resort, UK.

Ovation

See Charles Kaman.

Parklands

The house in Bowdon, Cheshire, which was both the base for the charity Ishval, and was, between the years 1964-1994, the home of Eugene Halliday and his wife Margaret, known as Peg.

David and Zero Mahlowe also shared the same house.

Pegasus Cases

The case shown on page 133 was made for the Stephan Schlemper 'Kompakt Guitar' by Sam Gifford at Pegasus Cases, Scotland UK. Email: sam@pegasus-cases.com

Philip Jones Brass Ensemble

See Philip Jones.

Purcell Room

Part of the Royal Festival Hall complex. It is situated in the Queen Elizabeth Hall building, and is the most intimate concert hall venue on site, making it especially suitable for chamber music which includes guitar recitals.

Ratcliffe, Ken (later Khen Ratcliffe)

1919 - 1992, was a Yoga teacher and co-founder with Eugene Halliday of the International Hermeneutic Society.

Resek, John

Violinist, formerly with the BBC Northern Symphony Orchestra (which became the BBC Philharmonic), working in the studio and traveling internationally with leading international artists which included Solti, Menuhin and Rostropovich. He now, as a freelance player, dedicates his time to making concerts as a soloist and performing with chamber music ensembles.

Rose, Philip and Elizabeth

Actors, puppeteers, artists, writers. Friends of Eugene Halliday who for many years had a successful business, the Rose Studio, making and selling plaster models, in Westward Ho!

Schillinger, Joseph

See text Chapter Seven.

Schlemper, Stephan

Luthier who made a Kompakt Classical Guitar for John Zaradin to facilitate flying with an instrument. The overall length of the guitar is less than a traditional classical model; a standard playing scale length is retained but the sizes of the body and head are reduced.

Stephan Schlemper prepares his guitars with the possibility of including a radio system with microphones and/or pickups built into the guitar. He combines the traditional guitar construction with electronics, needed for varied professional traveling and playing.

Stephan adds:

"All my concern as a luthier has been to contribute to the success of the musician. The guitar without the musician is nothing, but good music is made when the guitar responds to the feelings and expressions of the player.

"After John got his first Schlemper-System Classical Guitar he found that it could be used in both solo and in ensemble settings and also, that he did not have to compromise and use a less 'acoustic' instrument even when playing with large orchestras and percussion sections.

"However, he than explained to me the daily life of the air travelling guitarist and the problems of getting the instrument into the cabin.

"The 'Classic Kompact' was born - with a sound that projected, in ensembles, better than the normal Classic model. Happy to see the right instruments in the right hands."

Scott, Cyril Meir

1879–1970. English composer, writer, and poet. He had a long artistic association with the pianist Evelyn Suart (Lady Harcourt), who championed his music and premièred many of his works. She was a Christian Scientist, and it was through her that Scott developed his interest in metaphysics.

Scriabin, Alexander Nikolayevich

1872 - 1915. Russian Symbolist composer and pianist with early work much influenced by Frédéric Chopin. He developed an interest in atonal systems and synesthesia, relating sound and color. His color-coded circle of fifths was derived from theosophical and mystic ideas which, although innovative, were controversial at the time. However, he attracted the attentions of both Igor Stravinsky and Sergei Prokofiev. Leo Tolstoy described his music as "a sincere expression of genius".

Segovia Torres, Andrés

1st Marquis of Salobreña, 1893 – 1987. Virtuoso Spanish classical guitarist from Linares, Spain, who established the guitar as an international concert instrument. He inspired non-guitar playing composers to write for the instrument and, with his own arrangements of established music, laid a foundation for a substantial and varied modern repertoire.

Shakespeare, William

1564 - 1616. Was an English poet, playwright and actor, widely regarded as the greatest writer in the English language and the world's pre-eminent dramatist. He is often called England's national poet and the 'Bard of Avon'. His extant works, including some collaborations, consist of about 38 plays, 154 sonnets, two long narrative poems, and a few other verses, the authorship of some of which is uncertain. His plays have been translated into every major living language and are performed more often than those of any other playwright.

Socrates

470/469 BC – 399 BC. Classical Greek (Athenian) philosopher, credited as one of the founders of Western philosophy. He is an enigmatic figure known chiefly through the accounts of classical writers, especially those of his students Plato and Xenophon and the plays of his contemporary Aristophanes. Plato's dialogues are among the most comprehensive accounts of Socrates to survive from antiquity.

Voice leading chart

Shows how notes move correctly according to a musical grammar.

Wellington Road

The road in Whalley Range, Manchester, where Eugene Halliday and many of his friends lived from the 1940s through to the 1960s and beyond. The houses, numbered 9 and 33, were homes to many artists and musicians, among others.

Yohannan, Hephzibah

Editor of the Halliday Review, former trustee of Ishval, founder member of the Eugene Halliday Association, Aikido practitioner and gardener. Email: info@ehassociation.org

Zaradin, John

For full details, see johnzaradin.com where free dowloads of selected recordings are offered.

Zaradin, Noëlle

Artist and wife of John Zaradin. Deceased November 2013.

♃ ♄ ☿

ACKNOWLEDGEMENTS

We would like to acknowledge and thank everyone who has actively contributed to the creation of this book, including Jon Cook (UEA) and Ben Galley (Shelf Help) through their Guardian Masterclasses, also Bob Hardy.

We would like to include a special appreciation for our proof readers: Richard Freeman, Chris Shepherd & Chas White (Carel Press), Russell Haynes, Jon Hudson, John Resek and Barbara Pidgeon.

Also, to Robin Miksad who, sacrificed many mornings in Skyping to Europe from her coffee and toast breakfast table in the Blue Ridge Mountains, Virginia, to chew on the nuances of 'international English' and offer clarifications and recommendations.

Finally, to all who have permitted the use of visuals and photographs.

Every effort has been made to credit creators of all material reproduced in this book. If we have inadvertently made any omissions please contact the publishers who will be pleased to provide acknowledgement in future editions.

John Zaradin & Hephzibah Yohannan

The Authors

John Zaradin Personal Journey lets John Zaradin tell of his being introduced, at nineteen years of age, to the artist and writer Eugene Halliday, who was attracting musicians, actors and other artists and writers to work together on personal development. We see how John Zaradin was taught to become the guitarist/composer that he wanted to be. He explains that he sensed, even at a young age, that personal freedom was an important aspect of life and found, in his relationships with Eugene Halliday and friends, that he was learning how to work towards such a freedom. He began to understand that accepting the reality of his own thinking, feeling and willing, and working with it, could offer him a way to organize his life and live it in a more balanced way. He learned also that, no matter what field he might be involved in, good will orientation towards others with a will to equilibrate himself would better serve the cause of freedom and joy in life. John Zaradin is currently living in Albi, in south-west France.

Hephzibah Yohannan This book, *Personal Journey* grew out of a conversation which took place over a weekend in May 2014, between John Zaradin and Hephzibah Yohannan. They had not met for many years, and during the conversation Hephzibah learned of John Zaradin's path through life and how he has applied the principles he learned from Eugene Halliday. Hephzibah grew up within the community around Eugene; art, music, theatre and mythology were part of her education, along with the usual school subjects. A degree in Philosophy led to a gradual realisation that she needed to digest the ideas she had been absorbing, in order to understand and benefit from them. She found that they gave her an ability to 'place' the ideas and experiences which she met in life. They have enabled her to remember to balance and centre herself, while partaking in the whirligig of life. She agrees that a feeling of good will to others is key to the continual regaining of that balance which, however many times it is lost, can be found again, leading towards internal freedom. She lives in Manchester UK.